WeightWatchers®

Easy recipes cooked in one pot

One Pot Wonders

First published in Great Britain by Simon & Schuster UK Ltd, 2013
A CBS Company

Copyright © 2013, Weight Watchers International, Inc.
Simon & Schuster Illustrated Books, Simon & Schuster UK Ltd,
First Floor, 222 Gray's Inn Road, London WC1X 8HB

www.simonandschuster.co.uk

Simon & Schuster Australia, Sydney
Simon & Schuster India, New Delhi

Weight Watchers, **ProPoints** and the **ProPoints** icon are the registered
trademarks of Weight Watchers International Inc and are used under license
by Weight Watchers (UK) Ltd.

Weight Watchers Publications: Jane Griffiths, Linda Palmer and Nina McKerlie.

Recipes written by: Sue Ashworth, Sue Beveridge, Tamsin Burnett-Hall,
Cas Clarke, Siân Davies, Roz Denny, Nicola Graimes, Becky Johnson,
Kim Morphew, Joy Skipper, Penny Stephens and Wendy Veale as well
as Weight Watchers Leaders and Members.

Photography by: Iain Bagwell, Steve Baxter, Steve Lee, Juliet Piddington
and William Shaw.
Project editor: Nicki Lampon.
Design and typesetting: Martin Lampon.

Colour reproduction by Dot Gradations Ltd, UK.
Printed and bound in China.

A CIP catalogue for this book is available from the British Library

ISBN 978 1 47111 088 7

1 2 3 4 5 6 7 8 9 10

Pictured on the title page: Rosemary roast chicken p20.
Pictured on the Introduction: Lancashire hotpot p54, Salmon en croûte p92, Stir-fried
pork with baby corn p68.

WeightWatchers®

Easy recipes cooked in one pot

One Pot Wonders

SIMON &
SCHUSTER
ILLUSTRATED

London · New York · Sydney · Toronto · New Delhi

A CBS COMPANY

Weight Watchers **ProPoints** Weight Loss System is a simple way to lose weight. As part of the Weight Watchers **ProPoints** plan you'll enjoy eating delicious, healthy, filling foods that help to keep you feeling satisfied for longer and in control of your portions.

Ⓥ This symbol denotes a vegetarian recipe and assumes that, where relevant, free range eggs, vegetarian cheese, vegetarian virtually fat free fromage frais, vegetarian low fat crème fraîche and vegetarian low fat yogurts are used. Virtually fat free fromage frais, low fat crème fraîche and low fat yogurts may contain traces of gelatine so they are not always vegetarian. Please check the labels.

❄ This symbol denotes a dish that can be frozen. Unless otherwise stated, you can freeze the finished dish for up to 3 months. Defrost thoroughly and reheat until the dish is piping hot throughout.

Recipe notes

Egg size: Medium sized, unless otherwise stated.

Raw eggs: Only the freshest eggs should be used. Pregnant women, the elderly and children should avoid recipes with eggs that are not fully cooked or raw.

All fruits and vegetables: Medium sized, unless otherwise stated.

Stock: Stock cubes are used in recipes, unless otherwise stated. These should be prepared according to packet instructions.

Recipe timings: These are approximate and meant to be guidelines. Please note that the preparation time includes all the steps up to and following the main cooking time(s).

Microwaves: Timings and temperatures are for a standard 800 W microwave. If necessary, adjust your own microwave.

Low fat spread: Where a recipe states to use a low fat spread, a light spread with a fat content of no less than 38% should be used.

Low fat soft cheese: Where low fat soft cheese is specified in a recipe, this refers to soft cheese with a fat content of less than 5%.

Contents

Introduction

Cooking from scratch can leave you with a kitchen full of bowls, plates, pans and dishes to clear up afterwards. It's no wonder creating tasty, healthy, home-cooked meals can sometimes seem like a chore. *One Pot Wonders* is here to help, packed full of recipes from the best of Weight Watchers cookbooks. Simple to follow, it's all about easy cooking using just one main pan, dish or pot.

For midweek suppers, tempt your family and friends with Stir-fried Pork with Baby Corn, Goat's Cheese and Lentil Stuffed Peppers or Turkey Pilaff. If you have more time, try a one pot roast, like Rosemary Roast Chicken or Pot Roast Mustard Beef. There are even simple desserts included, such as Slow Roasted Plums and Apple Bread Pudding. *One Pot Wonders* is here to make your life easier, and it will help save on the washing up too.

About Weight Watchers

For more than 40 years Weight Watchers has been helping people around the world to lose weight using a long term sustainable approach. Weight Watchers successful weight loss system is based on four tried and trusted principles:

- Eating healthily
- Being more active
- Adjusting behaviour to help weight loss
- Getting support in weekly meetings

Our unique ***ProPoints*** system empowers you to manage your food plan and make wise recipe choices for a healthier, happier you.

To find out more about Weight Watchers and the ***ProPoints*** values for these recipes contact Customer Service on 0845 345 1500.

Storing and freezing

Making meals ahead of time and storing and freezing them is one of the keys to producing healthy tasty meals during a busy week. Many dishes store well in the fridge, but make sure you use them up within a day or two. Some can also be frozen. Try making double the quantity when you cook a recipe and storing the extra portions in the freezer. This way you'll always have a fantastic selection of meals that you can pull out and reheat at the end of a busy day. However, it is important to make sure you know how to freeze safely.

- Wrap any food to be frozen in rigid containers or strong freezer bags. This is important to stop foods contaminating each other or getting freezer burn.
- Label the containers or bags with the contents and date – your freezer should have a star marking that tells you how long you can keep different types of frozen food.
- Never freeze warm food – always let it cool completely first.
- Never freeze food that has already been frozen and defrosted.
- Freeze food in portions, then you can take out as little or as much as you need each time.
- Defrost what you need in the fridge, making sure you put anything that might have juices, such as meat, on a covered plate or in a container.
- Fresh food, such as raw meat and fish, should be wrapped and frozen as soon as possible.
- Most fruit and vegetables can be frozen by open freezing. Lay them out on a tray, freeze until solid and then pack them into bags.
- Some vegetables, such as peas, broccoli and broad beans, can be blanched first by cooking for 2 minutes in boiling water. Drain, refresh under cold water and then freeze once cold.

- Fresh herbs are great frozen – either seal leaves in bags or, for soft herbs such as basil and parsley, chop finely and add to ice cube trays with water. These are great for dropping into casseroles or soups straight from the freezer.

Some things cannot be frozen. Whole eggs do not freeze well, but yolks and whites can be frozen separately. Vegetables with a high water content, such as salad leaves, celery and cucumber, will not freeze. Fried foods will be soggy if frozen, and sauces such as mayonnaise will separate when thawed and should not be frozen.

Shopping hints and tips

Always buy the best ingredients you can afford. If you are going to cook healthy meals, it is worth investing in some quality ingredients that will really add flavour to your dishes. When buying meat, choose lean cuts of meat or lean mince, and if you are buying precooked sliced meat, buy it fresh from the deli counter.

When you're going around the supermarket it's tempting to pick up foods you like and put them in your trolley without thinking about how you will use them. So, a good plan is to decide what dishes you want to cook before you go shopping, check your store cupboard and make a list of what you need. You'll save time by not drifting aimlessly around the supermarket picking up what you fancy.

We've added a checklist here for some of the storecupboard ingredients used in this book. Just add fresh ingredients in your regular shop and you'll be ready to cook the wonderful recipes in *One Pot Wonders*.

Store cupboard checklist

- [ ] almonds (ground and flaked)
- [ ] artichokes, canned
- [ ] artificial sweetener
- [ ] bay leaves
- [ ] beans, canned
- [ ] capers, in a jar
- [ ] caraway seeds
- [ ] cardamom pods
- [ ] cayenne pepper
- [ ] cherries, canned in syrup
- [ ] chick peas, canned
- [ ] chilli (flakes and powder)
- [ ] Chinese five spice
- [ ] chocolate, milk
- [ ] cinnamon (sticks and ground)
- [ ] cloves, ground
- [ ] cocoa powder
- [ ] cooking spray, calorie controlled
- [ ] coriander (seeds and ground)
- [ ] cornflour
- [ ] cranberry sauce
- [ ] cumin (seeds and ground)
- [ ] curry powders
- [ ] custard, ready-made
- [ ] fish sauce
- [ ] flour, plain white
- [ ] garam masala
- [ ] herbs, dried
- [ ] honey, clear
- [ ] jelly, sugar free
- [ ] lentils (dried and canned)
- [ ] mustard (Dijon and wholegrain)
- [ ] mustard seeds
- [ ] noodles, dried
- [ ] oats, porridge
- [ ] oil (olive and sunflower)
- [ ] olives, stoned in a jar
- [ ] paprika
- [ ] pasta, dried
- [ ] peaches, canned in natural juice
- [ ] peppercorns
- [ ] pesto
- [ ] pineapple, canned in natural juice
- [ ] rice, dried
- [ ] saffron strands
- [ ] salt
- [ ] sardines, canned in brine
- [ ] sesame seeds
- [ ] soy sauce
- [ ] sponge fingers
- [ ] stock cubes
- [ ] sugar
- [ ] Tabasco sauce
- [ ] teriyaki marinade
- [ ] tomato purée
- [ ] tomatoes, canned
- [ ] tomatoes, sun-dried
- [ ] turmeric
- [ ] vanilla extract
- [ ] vinegars
- [ ] Worcestershire sauce

Perfect poultry

Turkey meatball broth

Serves 4
335 calories per serving
Takes 30 minutes
❄

500 g (1 lb 2 oz) lean minced
  turkey
2 tablespoons finely shredded
  fresh basil leaves
grated zest of ½ a lemon
25 g (1 oz) Parmesan cheese,
  grated
calorie controlled cooking
  spray
1 onion, chopped finely
2 carrots, peeled and diced
2 celery sticks, sliced
2 garlic cloves, crushed
1 tablespoon tomato purée
410 g can chick peas, drained
  and rinsed
600 ml (20 fl oz) hot chicken
  stock
salt and freshly ground black
  pepper

The secret to this delicious supper is to brown the meatballs to give the broth maximum flavour. Serve with a 50 g (1¾ oz) chunk of crusty bread per person.

1 Mix together the minced turkey, basil, lemon zest, cheese and seasoning in a bowl. With wet hands, create 16 small meatballs.

2 Spray a deep, wide, non stick saucepan with the cooking spray and cook the meatballs for 5 minutes, turning until browned all over. Remove and set aside.

3 Spray the pan again with the cooking spray and add the onion, carrots, celery and garlic. Cook for 3 minutes until beginning to soften. Add the tomato purée and cook for 30 seconds longer. Stir in the chick peas and stock and return the meatballs. Bring to a simmer and cook for 8–10 minutes until the vegetables are tender and the meatballs are cooked. Check the seasoning and serve.

Teriyaki chicken skewers

Serves 2
240 calories per serving
Takes 30 minutes +
   marinating

6 tablespoons teriyaki sauce
**4 skinless boneless chicken
   thighs, cut into chunky
   pieces**
**10 chestnut or shiitake
   mushrooms, halved through
   the stalk**
**6 spring onions, cut into 4 cm
   (1½ inch) lengths**

*Ready-made teriyaki sauce gives chicken plenty of flavour
and is available in most supermarkets. It has a consistency
similar to soy sauce.*

1 Pour the teriyaki sauce into a large plastic food bag and
place inside a bowl to avoid spillage.

2 Put the chicken pieces in the bag, along with the
mushrooms and spring onions. Squeeze the excess air out of
the bag and seal tightly. All of the ingredients should now be in
close contact with the sauce. Marinate in the fridge for at least
1 hour.

3 Soak four wooden skewers in cold water for at least
10 minutes to prevent them from burning during cooking.

4 Preheat the grill to high and line the grill pan with foil.
Thread the chicken and vegetables on to the skewers. Grill for
12–15 minutes, turning occasionally and brushing with the
marinade.

Ⓥ **Variation...** For a vegetarian alternative, replace the
chicken with 300 g (10½ oz) Quorn Chicken Style Pieces.
These will only take around 8 minutes to cook under the
grill.

One dish baked brunch

Serves 4

222 calories per serving

Takes 5 minutes to prepare,
20 minutes to cook

calorie controlled cooking
  spray

3 medium slices wholemeal
  bread

3 teaspoons low fat spread

4 turkey rashers, snipped
  roughly

100 g (3½ oz) mushrooms,
  quartered

150 g (5½ oz) cherry
  tomatoes, halved

4 eggs

150 ml (5 fl oz) skimmed milk

salt and freshly ground black
  pepper

This all-in-one cooked brunch is very easy to prepare and keeps your kitchen smelling lovely and fresh, as it's baked in the oven rather than cooked on the hob.

1 Preheat the oven to Gas Mark 5/190°C/fan oven 170°C. Lightly spray a 23 cm (9 inch) square baking dish with the cooking spray.

2 Spread the bread thinly with the low fat spread, cut each slice into four triangles and arrange around the edge of the dish, points uppermost. Scatter the turkey rashers, mushrooms and cherry tomatoes in the centre of the dish.

3 Beat the eggs and milk with some seasoning and then pour all over the other ingredients. Bake in the oven for 20 minutes until the egg mixture is set and the bread is crisp and toasted.

Rosemary roast chicken

Serves 4

282 calories per serving

Takes 15 minutes to prepare + 15 minutes resting, 1¼ hours to cook

1.75 kg (3 lb 14 oz) whole chicken

1 lemon, halved and juice squeezed into a bowl

2 fresh rosemary sprigs, plus 1 tablespoon chopped fresh rosemary

calorie controlled cooking spray

500 g (1 lb 2 oz) new potatoes, scrubbed and halved

350 g (12 oz) Chantenay carrots, scrubbed and trimmed

3 leeks, each cut into 6 chunks

salt and freshly ground black pepper

Roasting the chicken breast side down helps to keep the breast meat moist.

1 Preheat the oven to Gas Mark 6/200°C/fan oven 180°C. Wipe the chicken inside and out with kitchen towel. Tuck the squeezed lemon halves and rosemary sprigs inside the chicken cavity. Season the chicken and spray with the cooking spray. Sit in a large roasting tin, breast side down. Roast for 30 minutes.

2 Toss together the potatoes, carrots and leeks and spray with the cooking spray. Add to the roasting tin around the chicken. Roast for 30 minutes, stirring the vegetables halfway through.

3 Turn the chicken breast side up and pour the lemon juice over the chicken and vegetables. Scatter with the chopped rosemary, stir the vegetables again and return to the oven for 15 minutes.

4 Remove the chicken from the oven and let it rest for 15 minutes, loosely covered with foil. Transfer the vegetables to a dish and keep warm. Remove the skin and carve the chicken, serving four 45 g (1½ oz) slices per person, with the vegetables.

Turkey pilaff

Serves 4
211 calories per serving
Takes 30 minutes
❄

calorie controlled cooking
   spray
**500 g (1 lb 2 oz) skinless
boneless turkey breast, cut
into bite size pieces**
1 small onion, chopped finely
1 carrot, peeled and diced
1 leek, sliced
1 celery stick, sliced
1 apple, cored and diced
1 cinnamon stick
½ teaspoon ground cloves
4 cardamom pods
100 ml (3½ fl oz) hot chicken
   stock
410 g can green lentils,
   drained and rinsed
1 tablespoon finely chopped
   fresh parsley
salt and freshly ground black
   pepper

*Serve with a baby spinach, rocket and watercress salad,
tossed with 2 tablespoons of fat free salad dressing per
person.*

1 Heat a wide, lidded, non stick pan and spray with the
cooking spray. Add the turkey pieces and cook for 3 minutes,
stirring until brown all over.

2 Reduce the heat and stir in the onion, carrot, leek, celery,
apple, cinnamon stick, cloves and cardamom pods. Cover and
cook for 5 minutes until the vegetables are starting to soften,
stirring occasionally.

3 Pour in the stock, bring to a simmer, cover and cook
for 5 minutes. Add the lentils and cook gently for a further
5 minutes until the turkey is cooked.

4 Remove the cinnamon stick and discard. Stir in the parsley,
season and serve immediately.

Ⓥ **Variation...** For a vegetarian version, replace the turkey
with a 350 g packet of Quorn Chicken Style Pieces and
replace the chicken stock with vegetable stock.

Mexican turkey casserole

Serves 4

419 calories per serving

Takes 25 minutes to prepare,
50–60 minutes to cook

**calorie controlled cooking
spray**

**400 g (14 oz) skinless
boneless turkey breast,
cubed**

2 garlic cloves, crushed

1 large onion, sliced

**1 large red chilli, de-seeded
and chopped finely**

**1 teaspoon coriander seeds,
crushed**

**1 teaspoon cumin seeds,
crushed**

**600 ml (20 fl oz) chicken or
vegetable stock**

200 g (7 oz) dried brown rice

**400 g can chick peas, drained
and rinsed**

400 g can chopped tomatoes

1 large aubergine, diced

a small bunch of fresh
coriander, chopped

salt and freshly ground black
pepper

*A one pot meal full of vibrant Mexican flavours. Serve with
a medium soft flour tortilla per person.*

1 Heat a flameproof casserole dish on the hob and spray with
the cooking spray. Add the turkey, season and stir-fry for about
5 minutes until golden all over. Remove the turkey from the
dish and set aside.

2 Spray the casserole with the cooking spray again, add the
garlic, onion, chilli and spices and stir-fry for 4–5 minutes until
the onion has softened.

3 Return the turkey to the pan together with half the stock
and all the other ingredients except the coriander. Bring to the
boil and simmer for 50–60 minutes, topping up with stock as
necessary. Stir in the coriander and serve.

Quick and easy paella

Serves 4

340 calories per serving

Takes 15 minutes to prepare +
5 minutes standing,
20 minutes to cook

A real Weight Watchers classic, this will appeal to the whole family.

2 teaspoons sunflower or olive oil

2 lean back bacon rashers, chopped

150 g (5½ oz) skinless boneless chicken breast, chopped

1 onion, chopped

2 garlic cloves, crushed

1 small red pepper, de-seeded and chopped

1 tablespoon paprika

1 teaspoon turmeric

2 teaspoons dried marjoram

200 g (7 oz) dried risotto rice

850 ml (1½ pints) hot chicken stock

125 g (4½ oz) frozen peas, defrosted

salt and freshly ground black pepper

1 Heat the oil in a large, lidded, non stick frying pan and stir-fry the bacon and chicken for about 2 minutes. Add the onion, garlic and red pepper and continue cooking for about 3 minutes, stirring occasionally.

2 Mix in the paprika, turmeric, marjoram and rice and cook for 1 minute more.

3 Pour in the stock and bring to the boil, stirring well. It will look very wet but don't worry – risotto rice absorbs a lot of liquid. Season and turn the heat down to a simmer. Cover and cook gently for about 15 minutes or until all the liquid has been absorbed. While it is cooking, stir or shake the pan once only.

4 Add the peas and cook for another 3 minutes.

5 Remove from the heat and leave to stand, covered, for 5 minutes before serving.

Chicken and vegetable curry

Serves 4

265 calories per serving

Takes 25 minutes to prepare,
  1 hour to cook

❄

**calorie controlled cooking
  spray**

**350 g (12 oz) skinless
  boneless chicken breasts,
  diced**

1 onion, chopped

**225 g (8 oz) potatoes, peeled
  and diced**

**225 g (8 oz) carrots, peeled
  and sliced**

1 aubergine, diced

2 garlic cloves, crushed

**2 green chillies, de-seeded
  and chopped finely**

**3 tablespoons medium curry
  powder**

50 g (1¾ oz) dried red lentils

400 g can chopped tomatoes

300 ml (10 fl oz) chicken stock

**salt and freshly ground black
  pepper**

**2 tablespoons chopped fresh
  coriander, to garnish**

*This tastes even better the day after cooking, as the
flavours will have had time to develop.*

1 Heat a large, lidded, non stick frying pan and spray it with
the cooking spray. Add the chicken and stir-fry over a high heat
until it is evenly browned. Add the onion, potatoes, carrots,
aubergine, garlic, chillies and curry powder. Stir well so that all
the ingredients get an even coating of the curry powder. Cook
for 2 minutes.

2 Stir in the lentils, tomatoes, stock and seasoning and bring
to the boil. Reduce the heat, cover and simmer for 1 hour,
stirring from time to time.

3 Spoon into four warmed bowls and scatter with the
coriander to serve.

Chicken and mushroom risotto

Serves 4

415 calories per serving

Takes 15 minutes to prepare,
20 minutes to cook

❄

2 tablespoons olive oil

225 g (8 oz) dried risotto rice

225 g (8 oz) skinless boneless
chicken breast, chopped into
chunks

2 garlic cloves, crushed

1 onion, chopped

1 yellow or green pepper,
de-seeded and sliced

100 g (3½ oz) mushrooms,
sliced

2 teaspoons dried Italian
herbs

1 litre (1¾ pints) hot chicken
or vegetable stock

25 g (1 oz) sun-dried tomatoes
in olive oil, rinsed and sliced

salt and freshly ground black
pepper

To serve

4 tablespoons finely grated
Parmesan cheese

a few fresh basil sprigs

*Choose Italian Arborio rice and freshly grated Parmesan
cheese to make the best risotto; flavour is everything.
Children will like the creamy texture.*

1 Heat the oil in a large, lidded, non stick frying pan. Add the
rice and sauté gently for 2 minutes. Add the chicken and cook
gently for a further 2–3 minutes, stirring constantly.

2 Add the garlic, onion and pepper. Cook over a low heat,
stirring frequently, for 5 minutes. Add the mushrooms and
cook for another minute or so.

3 Stir in the dried herbs, half the stock and the sun-dried
tomatoes. Bring to the boil, reduce the heat, cover and simmer
gently for about 20 minutes, adding further stock as needed,
until the rice is tender and all the stock has been absorbed.

4 Season, ladle on to warmed plates and sprinkle each portion
with 1 tablespoon of Parmesan cheese. Garnish with the basil
sprigs.

Tip... If all the stock has been absorbed before the rice is
tender, add a little more stock or hot water.

Variations... For a special occasion, replace 150 ml (5 fl oz)
of the stock with 150 ml (5 fl oz) dry white wine.

You could add 2 skinned and chopped fresh tomatoes in
step 3, just 5 minutes before the end of the cooking time.

Chicken, Stilton and cranberry strudels

Serves 6

310 calories per serving

Takes 10 minutes to prepare,
20 minutes to cook

6 x 45 g (1½ oz) sheets filo
pastry, measuring
50 x 24 cm (20 x 9½ inches)

calorie controlled cooking
spray

6 tablespoons cranberry sauce

6 x 125 g (4½ oz) skinless
boneless chicken breasts

75 g (2¾ oz) Stilton cheese,
crumbled

freshly ground black pepper

*A superbly flavoursome recipe using just a handful of
ingredients, these strudels are very easy to prepare and
can be kept in the fridge until ready to bake.*

1 Preheat the oven to Gas Mark 6/200°C/fan oven 180°C.

2 Unroll the filo pastry, but keep the sheets in a stack so that
they don't dry out. For each strudel, spray a sheet of pastry with
the cooking spray and fold in half to give a square. Spray again
with the cooking spray and then place 1 tablespoon of cranberry
sauce near the centre of the top edge.

3 Sit a chicken breast on top, season with black pepper and
press one sixth of the Stilton on to the chicken. Fold in the
sides of the pastry and then roll up to enclose completely.
Repeat to make a total of six strudels.

4 Place the strudels on a non stick baking tray sprayed with
the cooking spray and bake for 20 minutes until golden brown
and crisp.

Herby chicken casserole

Serves 4

246 calories per serving

Takes 25 minutes to prepare,
1 hour to cook

❄

4 x 165 g (5¾ oz) skinless
boneless chicken breasts

1 tablespoon finely chopped
fresh tarragon

1 tablespoon finely chopped
fresh parsley

1 tablespoon snipped fresh
chives

calorie controlled cooking
spray

1 fennel bulb, chopped roughly

150 g (5½ oz) small Chantenay
carrots, scrubbed and
trimmed

6 whole garlic cloves, peeled

300 ml (10 fl oz) chicken stock

200 g (7 oz) low fat soft
cheese

freshly ground black pepper

*Succulent chicken in a light creamy sauce, perfect as a
midweek supper or as a meal with friends.*

1 Cut a pocket into the thickest part of each chicken breast.
Mix together the tarragon, parsley and chives. Season with
black pepper and fill each chicken pocket with some of the
herb mixture.

2 Heat a large, lidded, flameproof casserole dish and spray the
chicken with the cooking spray. Cook the chicken for 5 minutes
until browned all over. Remove and set aside.

3 Spray the casserole again with the cooking spray and
cook the fennel, carrots and garlic for 5–7 minutes, stirring
occasionally, until starting to soften and colour. Return the
chicken to the pan and pour in the chicken stock. Bring to the
boil, cover and simmer for 1 hour.

4 Remove the chicken and vegetables from the casserole
using a slotted spoon and transfer to a warm plate. Whisk the
soft cheese into the casserole and bring to the boil. Bubble
for 5–8 minutes until slightly reduced and thickened. Check
the seasoning, return the chicken and vegetables to the
casserole to warm and serve immediately.

Turkey jambalaya

Serves 4
440 calories per serving
Takes 55 minutes

**calorie controlled cooking
  spray**
2 large onions, chopped
1 celery stick, chopped
**1 green pepper, de-seeded and
  diced**
**225 g (8 oz) button
  mushrooms, sliced**
**500 g (1 lb 2 oz) skinless
  boneless turkey breast,
  diced**
**100 g (3½ oz) lean cooked
  ham, diced**
400 g can chopped tomatoes
150 ml (5 fl oz) tomato juice
1 teaspoon Tabasco sauce
2 bay leaves
2 garlic cloves, crushed
1 teaspoon cayenne pepper
**1 red chilli, de-seeded and
  chopped finely**
**225 g (8 oz) dried long grain
  rice**
425 ml (15 fl oz) chicken stock
**salt and freshly ground black
  pepper**

*Jambalaya is a spicy rice dish made with whatever meat
is available.*

1 Heat a large non stick frying pan and spray with the cooking
spray. Fry the onions for 4 minutes until softened.

2 Add the celery, green pepper and mushrooms and stir-fry
for 5 minutes. Add the turkey, ham, tomatoes, tomato juice,
Tabasco, bay leaves, garlic, cayenne, chilli and seasoning, stir
together and simmer for 15 minutes.

3 Add the rice and stock and cook for 15–20 minutes,
stirring every 5 minutes, until the rice is firm but slightly
moist and the stock is completely absorbed. Serve
immediately.

Sweet and sour chicken

Serves 2
372 calories per serving
Takes 20 minutes

calorie controlled cooking
  spray
2.5 cm (1 inch) fresh root
  ginger, grated
2 garlic cloves, sliced
2 x 150 g (5½ oz) skinless
  boneless chicken breasts,
  cut into bite size pieces
1 tablespoon cornflour
1 teaspoon Chinese five spice
200 g (7 oz) carrots, peeled
  and sliced thinly
a bunch of spring onions,
  sliced finely
100 g (3½ oz) sugar snap peas
  or mange tout
300 ml (10 fl oz) orange juice
1 tablespoon clear honey
1 tablespoon rice or white
  wine vinegar
2 tablespoons soy sauce
1 teaspoon sesame oil
salt and freshly ground black
  pepper

A quick, easy and tasty dish – perfect for a midweek supper.

1 Heat a wok or large non stick frying pan and spray with the cooking spray. Stir-fry the ginger and garlic for 2 minutes until golden and then add the chicken pieces. Stir-fry over a high heat for 5 minutes.

2 Mix the cornflour to a paste with 2 tablespoons of water and add to the pan with all the other ingredients. Cook until the sauce thickens and becomes glossy. Check the seasoning and serve at once.

Slow cooked chicken with mushrooms

Serves 4

200 calories per serving

Takes 15 minutes to prepare,
1½ hours to cook

❄

calorie controlled cooking
  spray

1 onion, chopped

2 garlic cloves, crushed

4 x 75 g (2¾ oz) skinless
  boneless chicken thighs

4 x 75 g (2¾ oz) chicken
  drumsticks, skinned

400 g can chopped tomatoes

1 tablespoon balsamic vinegar

300 ml (10 fl oz) chicken stock

350 g (12 oz) open cup
  mushrooms

salt and freshly ground black
  pepper

2 tablespoons torn fresh basil,
  to garnish

This recipe has a slightly Mediterranean feel to it. Serve it simply with a 5 cm (2 inch) piece of French stick for a delicious winter warmer.

1 Heat a large, lidded, non stick saucepan and spray with the cooking spray. Add the onion, garlic and chicken portions. Cook for 5 minutes, turning the chicken portions so that they are evenly browned all over.

2 Add the tomatoes, vinegar, stock and mushrooms. Season and bring to the boil. Reduce the heat, cover and simmer for 1½ hours, by which time the chicken should be very tender.

3 Scatter with the basil before serving.

Stuffed chicken breasts

Serves 4

170 calories per serving

Takes 10 minutes to prepare,
15 minutes to cook

**50 g (1¾ oz) smoked ham,
diced**

**2 teaspoons snipped fresh
chives**

**100 g (3½ oz) low fat soft
cheese**

**4 x 165 g (5¾ oz) skinless
boneless chicken breasts**

**calorie controlled cooking
spray**

**salt and freshly ground black
pepper**

A simple, classic recipe.

1 Preheat the oven to Gas Mark 6/200°C/fan oven 180°C.

2 Mix the ham, chives and some seasoning into the soft cheese.

3 Using a small sharp knife, make a pocket along the length
of each chicken breast, taking care not to cut right through. Fill
with the stuffing and then place the chicken breasts in a small
non stick roasting tin. Spray with a little cooking spray.

4 Roast for 15 minutes or until the chicken is cooked through;
the juices should run clear when the thickest part of the
chicken is pierced.

Lemon-glazed turkey with mange tout

Serves 2
180 calories per serving
Takes 15 minutes

225 g (8 oz) skinless boneless turkey breast, cut into strips
125 g (4½ oz) mange tout
2 spring onions, sliced
1 tablespoon clear honey
juice of ½ a lemon
1 tablespoon chopped fresh basil
1 teaspoon sesame seeds
salt and freshly ground black pepper

Serve, sizzling, stuffed into pitta bread pockets with loads of crisp salad leaves.

1 In a non stick frying pan, briskly dry-fry the turkey over a high heat for 3–4 minutes until the meat is well sealed and lightly coloured.

2 Add the mange tout and spring onions with 1–2 tablespoons of water if needed and stir-fry for a further 3–4 minutes. Add the honey, lemon juice, basil and sesame seeds. Season well.

3 Let the juices come to the boil, coating the turkey with the glaze that is forming. Serve immediately.

Chicken parcels

Serves 4
239 calories per serving
Takes 10 minutes to prepare,
40 minutes to cook

1 garlic clove, crushed
1 tablespoon fresh sage,
    chopped
2 tablespoons clear honey
1½ tablespoons wholegrain
    mustard
½ tablespoon olive oil
juice of a lemon
1 tablespoon soy sauce
4 x 165 g (5¾ oz) skinless
    boneless chicken breasts
8 lemon slices
8 fresh sage leaves
salt and freshly ground black
    pepper

This is a good recipe to use when you have guests, as you can prepare the parcels well in advance and leave them in the fridge until you are ready to cook them. This gives you more time to enjoy the company of your friends.

1 Preheat the oven to Gas Mark 5/190°C/fan oven 170°C. Prepare four pieces of foil, each large enough to wrap up a chicken breast.

2 In a screw top jar, shake together the garlic, sage, honey, mustard, oil, lemon juice and soy sauce. Season.

3 Score each chicken breast in a couple of places without cutting right through and place each breast on a piece of foil. Turn up the ends and sides of each piece of foil so that it can hold liquid and then pour on the sauce, dividing it equally between each breast. Top each with a slice of lemon and a fresh sage leaf. Seal the foil into parcels and bake in the oven for 40 minutes.

4 When cooked, open the parcels, lift out the chicken and place on warmed plates. Replace the sage leaves and lemon slices with fresh ones and use the sauce as gravy.

Tip... This is lovely served with Mediterranean-style roasted vegetables. The vegetables can be cooked in the oven alongside the chicken parcels, but put the vegetables in first as the oven temperature in this recipe is a little low, so they'll take an hour or so to roast.

Marvellous meat

Pork roast with ratatouille

Serves 4

315 calories per serving

Takes 20 minutes to prepare + resting, 1 hour to cook

1 kg (2 lb 4 oz) boneless pork shoulder joint, trimmed of visible fat

450 g (1 lb) vine ripened tomatoes, quartered or halved depending on size

2 red onions, cut into wedges

1 red pepper, de-seeded and cut into wedges

1 yellow or orange pepper, de-seeded and cut into wedges

4 garlic cloves, unpeeled

2 large courgettes, halved lengthways and cut into chunks

2 dessert apples, cored and cut into thick wedges

a few fresh rosemary or thyme sprigs

4 tablespoons soy sauce

200 ml (7 fl oz) vegetable stock

2 tablespoons Dijon mustard

150 g (5½ oz) virtually fat free plain fromage frais

salt and freshly ground black pepper

This makes an ideal alternative Sunday roast.

1 Preheat the oven to Gas Mark 4/180°C/fan oven 160°C. Sprinkle seasoning all over the skin of the pork and rub in.

2 Place all the vegetables, the apples and herbs in a roasting tin, sprinkle with the soy sauce and seasoning and toss together.

3 Place the pork joint on top of the vegetables and roast for 30 minutes. Toss the vegetables around, turn the pork and roast for another 30 minutes.

4 Remove from the oven and place the pork on a carving board for 10 minutes, covered with a piece of foil, to allow it to rest. Pour any fat off the vegetables, placing them in a serving bowl. Keep them warm.

5 Place the roasting tin on the hob. Add the vegetable stock and bring to the boil, scraping up any stuck on juices with a wooden spoon. Add the mustard, stir in and then remove from the heat and stir in the fromage frais. Serve the sauce with the vegetables and carved meat, serving 2 slices of pork per person.

One pot goulash

Serves 2
390 calories per serving
Takes 15 minutes to prepare,
1¾ hours to cook

❄

1 teaspoon caraway seeds

calorie controlled cooking
spray

250 g (9 oz) lean braising
steak, cubed

1 large onion, chopped

1 garlic clove, crushed

1 red pepper, de-seeded and
cut into chunks

½ teaspoon hot smoked
paprika (see Tip)

400 g can chopped tomatoes

100 ml (3½ fl oz) beef stock

300 g (10½ oz) new potatoes,
scrubbed and halved if large

1 tablespoon chopped fresh
dill (optional)

salt and freshly ground black
pepper

2 tablespoons low fat natural
yogurt, to serve

This is a great midweek dish as you can assemble it in advance up to the point where you put the casserole in the oven, and then just cook it when you need it. Dill isn't the traditional Hungarian accompaniment, but it is delicious with the tender, slow cooked beef.

1 Preheat the oven to Gas Mark 4/180°C/fan oven 160°C. Using a pestle and mortar or a heavy rolling pin, crush the caraway seeds to release their aroma. Set aside.

2 Spray a lidded flameproof casserole dish with the cooking spray and fry the beef for a few minutes until sealed and browned on all sides. Remove the beef from the pan and set aside.

3 If necessary, spray the pan again and then add the onion, garlic and pepper. Fry for 2–3 minutes to soften them. Return the beef to the pan and stir in the paprika, crushed caraway seeds, tomatoes, stock and potatoes.

4 Put the lid on the casserole dish, place it in the oven and cook for 1¾ hours or until the meat is tender. Stir occasionally.

5 Before serving, check the seasoning and stir in the chopped dill, if using. Divide between two large, warmed bowls and top each with a tablespoon of yogurt.

Tip... As the name suggests, hot smoked paprika is hotter than its milder counterpart and it adds a lovely smoky depth to this dish. If you use standard sweet paprika, use 2 teaspoons.

Chinese-style lamb

Serves 4

260 calories per serving

Takes 10 minutes to prepare,
35–40 minutes to cook

❄

450 g (1 lb) lean lamb neck
fillet, trimmed of visible fat
and cut into chunks

1 tablespoon chopped fresh
chives, to garnish

For the cooking liquid

5 cm (2 inch) strip lemon or
orange zest

50 ml (2 fl oz) soy sauce

2 tablespoons dry sherry

2 teaspoons light brown soft
sugar

2 spring onions, cut into 5 cm
(2 inch) pieces

2.5 cm (1 inch) fresh root
ginger, chopped

1 level teaspoon ground
cinnamon

East meets West in this tasty lamb dish.

1 Put all the ingredients for the cooking liquid in a
large, lidded, flameproof casserole dish or saucepan, add
125 ml (4 fl oz) of water and bring to the boil. Add the lamb,
cover, reduce the heat to a gentle simmer and cook for
35–40 minutes or until the meat is tender.

2 Remove the lamb to four individual plates to keep warm. Boil
the cooking juices rapidly until reduced by half. Strain over the
lamb and serve, garnished with the chives.

Tip... Fresh root ginger has a wonderful flavour and will
keep well in the fridge salad drawer for frequent use (it is
great in stir-fries and salad dressings). Alternatively, slice
or grate the ginger and store it in a re-sealable bag in the
freezer.

Variation... The cooking liquid is really versatile – try it with
duck, chicken or pork.

Beef rogan josh

Serves 4

290 calories per serving

Takes 25 minutes to prepare,
45 minutes to cook

❄

600 g (1 lb 5 oz) lean beef
brisket, trimmed of visible
fat and cubed

1 teaspoon hot chilli powder

calorie controlled cooking
spray

2 onions, sliced thinly

2 garlic cloves, chopped

4 cardamom pods, split

2 bay leaves

2 tablespoons rogan josh
curry powder

5 tablespoons canned
chopped tomatoes

150 g (5½ oz) low fat natural
yogurt

1 red chilli, de-seeded and
sliced, to garnish

This is just as tasty as any take-away version and much healthier.

1 Put the beef in a bowl with the chilli powder and turn the meat until coated.

2 Spray a large, lidded, non stick saucepan with the cooking spray and fry the onions for 7 minutes until softened, adding a splash of water if necessary to prevent them from sticking.

3 Spray the pan again with the cooking spray, toss in the beef and fry over a medium heat for 2 minutes until the meat is sealed and browned all over.

4 Add the garlic, cardamom pods, bay leaves and curry powder and cook, stirring, for 30 seconds. Add the tomatoes, yogurt and 1 litre (1¾ pints) of water and stir. Bring to the boil, reduce the heat and simmer, covered, for 45 minutes.

5 Remove the lid and cook, stirring occasionally, until the sauce has reduced and thickened. Serve topped with the sliced red chilli.

Lancashire hotpot

Serves 4

480 calories per serving

Takes 15 minutes to prepare,
2½ hours to cook

❄

calorie controlled cooking
spray

800 g (1 lb 11oz) potatoes,
peeled and sliced thinly

600 g (1 lb 5 oz) lamb cutlets,
trimmed of visible fat and
bones cleaned

3 onions, chopped finely

2 carrots, peeled and sliced

4 fresh thyme sprigs, chopped

1 bay leaf

a pinch of caster sugar

300 ml (10 fl oz) vegetable
stock

25 g (1 oz) low fat spread,
melted

salt and freshly ground black
pepper

*A traditional stew of lamb cutlets with thyme and a crisp
and golden potato topping.*

1 Preheat the oven to Gas Mark 3/170°C/fan oven 150°C.
Spray a lidded ovenproof dish with the cooking spray and put a
layer of potatoes in the bottom. Lay the cutlets on top.

2 Sprinkle in the onions, carrots and herbs, season well and
sprinkle with the sugar. Finish with the rest of the potatoes
arranged over the top so that the slices overlap one another.

3 Pour in the stock and brush the top with the melted low fat
spread. Cover and bake for 2½ hours, removing the lid for the
last 40 minutes so that the potatoes crisp up and brown.

Beef and shiitake mushroom stir-fry

Serves 2
248 calories per serving
Takes 20 minutes

100 g (3½ oz) tenderstem broccoli

225 g (8 oz) fillet steak, trimmed of visible fat and cut into thin strips

calorie controlled cooking spray

2 garlic cloves, sliced

25 g (1 oz) fresh root ginger, cut into matchsticks

100 g (3½ oz) shiitake mushrooms, sliced

½ red pepper, de-seeded and diced finely

50 ml (2 fl oz) teriyaki sauce

juice of a lime

The secret to a good stir-fry is to have all the ingredients prepared before you get cooking. That way everything cooks perfectly and retains some crunch.

1 Cut the florets from the broccoli stalks and set aside. Cut the broccoli stalks in half lengthways and then in half again to make short stems. Set aside.

2 Heat a wok or non stick frying pan until really hot. Spray the beef with the cooking spray and stir-fry for 5 minutes, stirring constantly, until brown. Remove and set aside. Spray the pan again, add the garlic and ginger and stir-fry for 1 minute.

3 Add the mushrooms, pepper, broccoli florets and stalks. Stir-fry for 3–4 minutes, stirring occasionally until just tender. Return the beef and add the teriyaki sauce. Remove from the heat, as it will bubble very quickly due to the heat of the pan. Pour over the lime juice, stir once more and serve immediately.

Ⓥ Variation... For a vegetarian version, replace the beef with 300 g (10½ oz) mixed mushrooms such as oyster, chestnut and portobello.

Thai-style red beef curry

Serves 4

195 calories per serving

Takes 20 minutes to prepare,
30 minutes to cook

❄

300 ml (10 fl oz) reduced fat
  coconut milk

2 tablespoons Thai red curry
  paste

2 tablespoons fish sauce

6 kaffir lime leaves

2.5 cm (1 inch) fresh root
  ginger, grated

1 garlic clove, crushed

350 g (12 oz) rump steak,
  trimmed of visible fat and
  cubed

175 g (6 oz) fine green beans,
  halved

175 g (6 oz) cherry tomatoes,
  halved

3 tablespoons chopped fresh
  coriander

*If this is too spicy for you, vary the amount of curry paste
according to your taste.*

1 Place the coconut milk in a large pan with the curry paste,
fish sauce, lime leaves, ginger and garlic. Heat for 5 minutes
until bubbling and then add the beef. Reduce the heat and
simmer for 20 minutes.

2 Add the green beans and cook for a further 10 minutes.

3 Toss in the cherry tomatoes and coriander and heat through.

Tip... Thai cookery uses fish sauce like the Chinese use soy
sauce. Most major supermarkets now stock it; look out for
it beside the soy sauce or in the ethnic food section.

Variation... You can also use sirloin steak if you wish.

Olive and lemon lamb chops

Serves 4

387 calories per serving

Takes 5 minutes to prepare
+ 20 minutes marinating,
20 minutes to cook

8 x 75 g (2¾ oz) lean lamb
chops, trimmed of visible fat

finely grated zest and juice of
a lemon

½ teaspoon dried chilli flakes

30 g (1¼ oz) stoned black
olives in brine, drained and
diced

2 tomatoes, de-seeded and
diced

calorie controlled cooking
spray

salt and freshly ground black
pepper

This is a quick and easy dinner party dish.

1 Season the lamb chops and place in a non metallic ovenproof dish. Mix together the lemon zest, lemon juice and chilli flakes and drizzle over the meat. Leave to marinate at room temperature for 20 minutes (see Tip).

2 Preheat the oven to Gas Mark 5/190°C/fan oven 170°C. Scatter the olives and diced tomatoes over the lamb, spray everything with the cooking spray and bake for 20 minutes until the meat is cooked through.

3 Serve the lamb with the olive and tomato topping and juices spooned over.

Tip... If marinating the chops for longer (up to 24 hours), cover with cling film and refrigerate.

French lamb casserole

Serves 4

285 calories per serving

Takes 15 minutes to prepare,
  2 hours to cook

✳

calorie controlled cooking
  spray

2 onions, chopped

3 garlic cloves, crushed

250 g (9 oz) lean cubed lamb

2 tablespoons tomato purée

400 g can chopped tomatoes

2 x 300 g cans haricot beans,
  drained and rinsed

2 fresh thyme sprigs

2 fresh majoram sprigs

2 fresh parsley sprigs

1 celery stick, chopped
  roughly

1 bay leaf

salt and freshly ground black
  pepper

a handful of chopped fresh
  parsley, to garnish

*This French dish cooks conveniently slowly in the oven
while you go and do something else.*

1 Preheat the oven to Gas Mark 4/180°C/fan oven 160°C.

2 Spray a lidded flameproof casserole dish with the cooking
spray and sauté the onions and garlic for 4 minutes on the
hob. Add a couple of tablespoons of water if necessary to
prevent them from sticking. Add the lamb and seal all over for
2 minutes.

3 Add the rest of the ingredients with 450 ml (16 fl oz) of water.
Cover and bake for 2 hours, stirring every now and then. Check
the seasoning and serve sprinkled with the parsley.

Quick classic pizza

Serves 2
315 calories per serving
Takes 20 minutes

**calorie controlled cooking
spray**
**23 cm (9 inch) ready-made
thin and crispy pizza base**

For the topping
**65 g ready-made tomato and
garlic pasta sauce**
**2 slices Parma ham, trimmed
of visible fat and halved
lengthways**
**10 stoned black olives in
brine, drained**
**50 g (1¾ oz) chestnut
mushrooms, sliced thinly**
**75 g (2¾ oz) mozzarella light,
torn into pieces**

One of the quickest pizzas ever.

1 Preheat the oven to Gas Mark 7/220°C/fan oven 200°C.
Spray a non stick baking tray with the cooking spray and then
put the pizza base on it.

2 Spread the base with the pasta sauce. Arrange the ham
slices around the base and then scatter over the olives,
mushrooms and mozzarella.

3 Bake for 10–12 minutes until the pizza base is browned
and the cheese is bubbling. Cut in half and serve immediately.

Pot roast mustard beef

Serves 4

327 calories per serving

Takes 20 minutes to prepare,
1¼ hours to cook

**calorie controlled cooking
spray**

**600 g (1 lb 5 oz) silverside
beef joint, trimmed of visible
fat**

2 onions, sliced thinly

2 garlic cloves, crushed

**1 tablespoon wholegrain
mustard**

**1 teaspoon dried oregano
or a small bunch of fresh
oregano, chopped**

4 carrots, peeled and chopped

**180 g (6 oz) parsnips, peeled
and chopped**

**300 ml (10 fl oz) beef or
vegetable stock**

2 bay leaves

1 tablespoon soy sauce

**1 tablespoon Worcestershire
sauce**

**salt and freshly ground black
pepper**

A flavoursome roast that is perfect for a Sunday lunch.

1 Preheat the oven to Gas Mark 4/180°C/fan oven 160°C.

2 Spray a large, lidded, flameproof casserole dish with the
cooking spray and, over a medium heat, brown the beef joint
on all sides. Season, remove the beef from the dish and set
aside.

3 Spray the dish again and stir-fry the onions and garlic for a
few minutes until the onions are softened, adding a splash of
water if necessary to prevent them from sticking.

4 Spread the mustard over the top of the beef and return it
to the casserole dish. Add all the other ingredients around the
beef, cover and cook in the oven for 1¼ hours.

5 Serve the beef sliced thinly with the roasted vegetables.

Rosemary lamb bake

Serves 2

390 calories per serving

Takes 15 minutes to prepare,
30 minutes to cook

200 g (7 oz) new potatoes,
scrubbed and halved

200 g (7 oz) carrots, peeled
and cut into chunks

1 red onion, cut into wedges

4 x 125 g (4½ oz) lamb leg
steaks, trimmed of visible fat

2 fresh rosemary sprigs

450 ml (16 fl oz) chicken or
vegetable stock

salt and freshly ground black
pepper

*A one pot roast, ready in under an hour, is great for
midweek suppers or even a casual Sunday lunch.*

1 Preheat the oven to Gas Mark 6/200°C/fan oven 180°C.

2 Place the potatoes, carrots and onion in a large non stick
roasting tin. Sprinkle with a little seasoning. Place the lamb
steaks and rosemary on top.

3 Pour over the stock and bake for 30 minutes until golden and
cooked through.

Variations... You can use the same quantity of lean pork
chops instead of the lamb.

For a change when using lamb or pork, add half a thinly
sliced lemon to the vegetables – it will cook in the stock and
give the juices extra flavour.

Stir-fried pork with baby corn

Serves 4
180 calories per serving
Takes 20 minutes

A super fresh and crunchy stir-fry, full of wonderful flavours and textures that makes a healthy and satisfying lunch or dinner.

calorie controlled cooking spray

300 g (10½ oz) pork fillet, trimmed of visible fat and sliced into 5 mm (¼ inch) thick medallions

4 carrots, peeled and cut into matchsticks

300 g (10½ oz) baby corn, halved lengthways

150 g (5½ oz) sugar snap peas, halved diagonally

2 tablespoons tomato purée

4 tablespoons soy sauce

2 garlic cloves, crushed

2.5 cm (1 inch) fresh root ginger, grated finely

1 tablespoon clear honey

2 tablespoons white, red or rice wine vinegar

salt and freshly ground black pepper

a small bunch of fresh chives or coriander, chopped, to garnish

1 Heat a wok or large non stick frying pan and spray with the cooking spray. Season and stir-fry the pork for 5 minutes, until golden brown and just cooked through.

2 Add the carrots, baby corn and sugar snap peas and stir-fry for another couple of minutes, until the vegetables are golden on the edges.

3 In a small bowl, whisk together all the other ingredients, except the chives or coriander, with 100 ml of cold water. Pour into the pan. Stir-fry for a further 2 minutes until the sauce is reduced and thickened. Serve scattered with the chives or coriander.

Toad in the hole

Serves 4

275 calories per serving

Takes 10 minutes to prepare,
40–45 minutes to cook

❄

125 g (4½ oz) plain white flour
1 egg
300 ml (10 fl oz) skimmed milk
calorie controlled cooking
spray
450 g (1 lb) reduced fat pork
sausages

This dish brings back childhood memories for so many people – and it's child's play itself to make.

1 Preheat the oven to Gas Mark 7/220°C/fan oven 200°C. Sift the flour into a large bowl and add the egg and half the milk.

2 Gradually stir in the flour, beating until smooth, and then stir in the rest of the milk.

3 Spray a shallow ovenproof dish with the cooking spray and arrange the sausages in it with a little space between each. Pour in the batter and cook for 40–45 minutes or until the batter is well risen and brown.

Keema curry

Serves 4

289 calories per serving

Takes 10 minutes to prepare,
30 minutes to cook

❄

500 g (1 lb 2 oz) extra lean
minced beef

1 onion, chopped finely

2 tablespoons medium curry
powder

400 g (14 oz) potatoes, peeled
and cut into 2.5 cm (1 inch)
dice

200 ml (7 fl oz) beef stock

400 g can chopped tomatoes

150 g (5½ oz) frozen peas

salt and freshly ground black
pepper

*Perfect for an easy Friday night supper served with
1 tablespoon low fat natural yogurt.*

1 Heat a large, lidded, non stick pan and brown the minced
beef and onion for 5 minutes, stirring frequently to break up the
meat. Add the curry powder and potatoes and fry for 1 minute
more.

2 Pour in the stock and tomatoes, season, cover and simmer
for 25 minutes.

3 Finally, mix in the peas and cook for a further 5 minutes until
tender.

Bacon and onion hotpot

Serves 2

371 calories per serving

Takes 15 minutes to prepare,
1¼ hours to cook

**500 g (1 lb 2 oz) potatoes,
peeled and sliced thinly**

1 large onion, sliced thinly

**500 ml (18 fl oz) chicken or
vegetable stock**

4 lean back bacon rashers

**salt and freshly ground black
pepper**

**2 tablespoons tomato ketchup,
to serve**

*This easy savoury bake has just four main ingredients, so
it's very economical.*

1 Preheat the oven to Gas Mark 5/190°C/fan oven 170°C.

2 Arrange the potato and onion slices in alternating layers in
a 1.5 litre (2¾ pint) baking or casserole dish, seasoning each
layer and finishing with a layer of potatoes. Pour in the stock.

3 Transfer to the oven and bake, uncovered, for 1 hour.
Arrange the bacon rashers on top and bake for another
15 minutes. The potatoes should be tender, and the top layer
of potatoes and the bacon should be crisp.

4 Serve on warmed plates with 1 tablespoon of tomato
ketchup for each portion.

Tip... If you have one, a shallow baking dish works better
than a deep one.

Moroccan lamb and green bean stir-fry

Serves 1

184 calories

Takes 10 minutes

calorie controlled cooking
  spray

**125 g (4½ oz) lean lamb leg
  steak, trimmed of visible fat
  and sliced thinly**

¼ teaspoon ground cumin

a pinch of ground cinnamon

**75 g (2¾ oz) green beans,
  halved**

1 ripe tomato, chopped
  roughly

freshly ground black pepper

This is a delicious, fragrant stir-fry.

1 Heat a lidded non stick frying pan until hot and spray with
the cooking spray. Season the lamb with black pepper and
stir-fry over a high heat for 3 minutes until browned.

2 Add the cumin and cinnamon, followed by the green beans,
tomato and 2 tablespoons of water. Cover the pan and cook
over a medium heat for 4–5 minutes, stirring once or twice,
until the beans are tender but still have a bit of crunch left.
Serve immediately.

Variation... Try using a 125 g (4½ oz) skinless chicken
breast fillet instead of the lamb.

Fantastic fish and seafood

Cajun spiced chowder

Serves 4
241 calories per serving
Takes 25 minutes

1 leek, sliced finely
1 celery stick, sliced finely
2 garlic cloves, crushed
400 ml (14 fl oz) hot fish stock
200 g (7 oz) potatoes, peeled and diced
198 g can sweetcorn, drained
1½ tablespoons Cajun spice blend
200 ml (7 fl oz) semi skimmed milk
150 g (5½ oz) smoked mackerel fillets, skin removed and flaked
salt and freshly ground black pepper

A truly satisfying winter warmer. Serve with a 50 g (1¾ oz) bread roll per person to dunk in the creamy soup.

1 Put the leek, celery, garlic, fish stock and potatoes into a large lidded saucepan. Bring to the boil, cover and simmer for 10 minutes.

2 Remove half the vegetables with a slotted spoon and reserve. Add half the sweetcorn, the Cajun spices and milk to the saucepan. Using a hand blender, whizz until smooth.

3 Add the remaining sweetcorn to the pan with the reserved vegetables. Gently heat to warm through. Check the seasoning and then divide between warmed bowls and scatter over the mackerel.

Prawn and butternut squash risotto

Serves 4

425 calories per serving

Takes 15 minutes to prepare, 25 minutes to cook

1 teaspoon olive oil

1 tablespoon tomato purée

1 tablespoon white wine vinegar

1 small onion, chopped

1 garlic clove, crushed

300 g (10½ oz) dried risotto rice

350 g (12 oz) butternut squash, peeled, de-seeded and cubed

850 ml (1½ pints) hot fish or chicken stock

175 g (6 oz) peeled cooked prawns, defrosted if frozen

2 tablespoons chopped fresh parsley

25 g (1 oz) Parmesan cheese, grated

salt and freshly ground black pepper

Quick and easy, risottos are perfect one pot meals.

1 In a large non stick pan, heat together the oil, tomato purée and vinegar. Stir in the onion and garlic and cook for 1 minute. Stir in the rice and squash and cook for 2 minutes.

2 Gradually add the stock a little at a time, waiting for it to be absorbed before adding more.

3 As you add the last of the stock, toss in the prawns, parsley and Parmesan. Continue cooking until the rice is just tender and has a creamy texture. Season to taste and serve at once.

Tip... Risotto is at its best when served immediately; this ensures that you get the creamy texture it is renowned for. When left to go cold, the rice will absorb any juices and become a little stodgy.

Variation... You can use the same amount of diced pumpkin or sweet potato instead of squash if you prefer.

Seafood stir-fry

Serves 2
161 calories per serving
Takes 10 minutes

1 teaspoon Sichuan
  peppercorns
½ teaspoon black peppercorns
calorie controlled cooking
  spray
1 red pepper, de-seeded and
  sliced
75 g (2¾ oz) mange tout
2 spring onions, sliced
  diagonally
2 garlic cloves, chopped finely
2.5 cm (1 inch) fresh root
  ginger, chopped finely
1 long red chilli, de-seeded
  and chopped finely
300 g (10½ oz) cooked
  seafood selection, defrosted
  if frozen
juice of ½ a lemon

This stir-fry uses a cooked seafood selection for speed and ease.

1 Toast the Sichuan peppercorns and black peppercorns in a dry wok or non stick frying pan over a medium-low heat, taking care not to burn them, until they smell aromatic and start to darken. Remove the spices from the wok or pan and crush them coarsely using a pestle and mortar or the end of a rolling pin.

2 Heat the wok or pan again and spray with the cooking spray. Add the red pepper and mange tout and stir-fry for 1 minute, adding a splash of water if necessary to prevent them from sticking.

3 Add the spring onions, garlic, ginger, chilli, toasted peppercorns and seafood. Stir-fry for 1 minute before squeezing in the lemon juice. Serve immediately.

Cod and leek parcels

Serves 4

140 calories per serving

Takes 15 minutes to prepare,
20 minutes to cook

**4 x 125 g (4½ oz) skinless cod
fillets**

**2 leeks, halved lengthways
and sliced**

**grated zest and juice of a
lemon**

2 teaspoons olive oil

**salt and freshly ground black
pepper**

A fresh-tasting, quick supper.

1 Preheat the oven to Gas Mark 4/180°C/fan oven 160°C.
Prepare four pieces of non stick baking parchment about
30 cm (12 inches) square and place a piece of fish in the
centre of each.

2 Share the other ingredients between the four fillets so that
each is evenly covered with leeks, lemon zest, lemon juice,
seasoning and a dribble of oil.

3 Scrunch up the baking parchment to make sealed parcels
and place on a baking tray. Bake for 20 minutes and serve in
the paper for each person to open their own.

Variation... Try salmon, haddock or coley instead of the cod.

Seafood paella

Serves 4

344 calories per serving

Takes 15 minutes to prepare,
25 minutes to cook

**a large pinch of saffron
strands**

2 tablespoons boiling water

1 teaspoon olive oil

1 small onion, chopped finely

1 garlic clove, crushed

**1 red pepper, de-seeded and
diced**

225 g (8 oz) dried risotto rice

**850 ml (1½ pints) fish or
vegetable stock**

125 g (4½ oz) frozen peas

**225 g (8 oz) skinless cod fillet,
cut into bite size pieces**

**2 tablespoons chopped fresh
parsley**

**125 g (4½ oz) cooked peeled
prawns, defrosted if frozen,
plus 4 still in their shells to
serve**

**salt and freshly ground black
pepper**

This looks impressive – perfect for a midweek meal.

1 Place the saffron in a small dish and cover with the boiling water. Leave to stand so that the saffron infuses and colours the water bright yellow.

2 Heat the oil in a large non stick frying pan and add the onion and garlic. Cook over a low heat, stirring, until the onion has softened but not browned.

3 Add the red pepper and rice to the pan together with the saffron, its soaking liquid and the stock. Bring to the boil and simmer for 15 minutes, until most of the liquid has been absorbed.

4 Add the peas and cod and continue cooking for 5 minutes. Mix in the parsley and peeled prawns, season to taste and cook for a further 2–3 minutes until piping hot. Serve with the unshelled prawns placed on top of the paella.

Pesto tuna

Serves 4
285 calories per serving
Takes 15 minutes

4 x 150 g (5½ oz) tuna steaks
30 g (1¼ oz) pesto
lemon wedges, to serve

For the salsa
250 g (9 oz) cherry tomatoes,
quartered
1 red onion, chopped finely
a bunch of fresh basil,
chopped roughly
1 tablespoon balsamic vinegar
2 teaspoons olive oil
salt and freshly ground black
pepper

Pesto infuses fresh tuna steaks with a delicious basil flavour, perfectly complemented by a cherry tomato salsa for a touch of the 'Olé'.

1 Mix all the salsa ingredients together in a bowl and set aside. Preheat the grill to medium.

2 Spread each tuna steak with a little pesto on one side, place pesto side up on a piece of foil on the grill pan and grill for 4 minutes. Turn the steaks over, spread the other side with more of the pesto and grill for another 4 minutes until cooked through.

3 Serve immediately with the salsa and lemon wedges to squeeze over.

Variation... For a fiery alternative, try spreading each tuna steak with a teaspoon of sweet chilli sauce instead.

Chilli prawn kebabs

Serves 4

220 calories per serving

Takes 20 minutes +
30 minutes marinating

1 tablespoon sesame or
stir-fry oil

3 tablespoons soy sauce

2 tablespoons lime or lemon
juice

1 tablespoon chopped fresh
mint or coriander

1 teaspoon finely grated fresh
root ginger

2 tablespoons hot chilli sauce

½ teaspoon Chinese five spice

1 yellow pepper, de-seeded
and cut into chunks

1 courgette, sliced

350 g (12 oz) large, peeled,
cooked prawns, defrosted
if frozen

350 g (12 oz) firm tofu, cut
into chunks

salt and freshly ground black
pepper

To garnish

lime or lemon wedges
(optional)

fresh mint or coriander sprigs
(optional)

Ideal for a summer barbecue.

1 In a shallow non metallic dish, mix together the oil, soy sauce, lime or lemon juice, mint or coriander, ginger, chilli sauce, Chinese five spice and seasoning. Soak twelve wooden kebab sticks in water for 10 minutes.

2 Thread the vegetables, prawns and tofu evenly on to the twelve wooden kebab sticks and then lay them in the marinade, turning to coat them on all sides. Cover and leave to marinate for at least 30 minutes, turning occasionally.

3 Preheat the grill. Arrange the kebabs on the grill rack and cook for 4–5 minutes, turning often and basting them with the marinade. Alternatively, cook over barbecue coals in the summer.

4 Serve at once, allowing three kebabs per person, garnished with lime or lemon wedges and mint or coriander sprigs, if using.

Balsamic monkfish

Serves 2

130 calories per serving

Takes 15 minutes to prepare,
25 minutes to cook

❄

**225 g (8 oz) skinless thick
monkfish fillet**

finely grated zest of a lemon

½ teaspoon dried tarragon

**15 g (½ oz) thinly sliced Parma
ham (about 2 slices)**

1 teaspoon olive oil

1 tablespoon balsamic vinegar

**225 g (8 oz) cherry tomatoes
on the vine**

**salt and freshly ground black
pepper**

A perfect dish for an intimate dinner for two.

1 Preheat the oven to Gas Mark 6/200°C/fan oven 180°C.

2 Rinse the monkfish and pat dry with kitchen towel. Make a horizontal split almost all the way through the fish.

3 Mix together the lemon zest, tarragon and a little seasoning. Spread into the slit of the fish. Use the Parma ham to wrap around the fish and then lift it into a non stick roasting tin.

4 Mix together the olive oil and balsamic vinegar and brush over the fish. Roast in the oven for 15 minutes. Arrange the tomatoes around the fish and return to the oven for 10 minutes.

5 To serve, transfer the tomatoes to warmed serving plates. Thinly carve the fish diagonally and arrange in a slightly fanned pattern next to the tomatoes. Drizzle over any juices left in the roasting tin.

Sardine and bean stew

Serves 4

290 calories per serving

Takes 10 minutes to prepare,
25 minutes to cook

calorie controlled cooking
spray

2 onions, chopped

2 garlic cloves, chopped

2 teaspoons ground cumin

2 x 400 g cans chopped
tomatoes

1 small red chilli, de-seeded
and chopped finely (optional)

2 x 120 g cans sardines in
brine, drained, rinsed and
patted dry

2 x 400 g cans borlotti beans,
drained and rinsed

a small bunch of fresh
coriander or parsley
(optional)

salt and freshly ground black
pepper

*A very quick and easy supper dish made from
storecupboard ingredients.*

1 Heat a large non stick frying pan and spray with the cooking
spray. Fry the onions and garlic for 5 minutes until softened,
adding a splash of water if necessary to prevent them from
sticking.

2 Add the cumin, tomatoes and chilli, if using, bring to the boil
and simmer for 20 minutes until thick.

3 Add the sardines and beans and check the seasoning.
Simmer for a further 5 minutes and then stir through the
coriander or parsley, if using, and serve.

Variation... You could use cannellini beans instead of the
borlotti beans.

Salmon en croûte

Serves 4

395 calories per serving

Takes 20 minutes to prepare,
30–35 minutes to cook

❄

calorie controlled cooking
spray

6 x 45 g (1½ oz) sheets filo
pastry, measuring
50 x 24 cm (20 x 9½ inches)

2 tablespoons plain white
flour

4 x 140 g (5 oz) skinless
salmon fillets (do not use
steaks)

60 g (2 oz) low fat soft cheese
with garlic and herbs

finely grated zest of a lemon

4 teaspoons chopped fresh dill
or parsley

salt and freshly ground black
pepper

*Fresh salmon fillets wrapped and baked in sheets of filo
pastry make a really special meal.*

1 Preheat the oven to Gas Mark 4/180°C/fan oven 160°C.
Lightly spray a non stick baking tray with the cooking spray.

2 Take a sheet of filo pastry, spray it 3–4 times with the
cooking spray and then lay another sheet on top. Spray the
second sheet in the same way and then place a third sheet
on top and spray yet again. Cut this stack in half widthways.
Repeat the process with the remaining sheets to give you four
piles of filo pastry.

3 Sprinkle the flour on to a plate and season. Rinse the salmon
fillets and pat them dry with kitchen towel. Check that there
are no bones and then dip them in the flour, patting off any
excess.

4 Place a piece of floured fish in the middle of each pile of
pastry and then spoon an equal amount of soft cheese on top
of each fillet. Spread it over the surface and sprinkle the lemon
zest and herbs on top. Season lightly.

5 Fold the filo pastry over the fillets to make parcels, tucking
in the ends. Lift the parcels on to the baking tray and lightly
spray them with the cooking spray. Bake them in the oven for
30–35 minutes, until the pastry is golden.

Variation... Try using trout fillets or sea bass instead of the
salmon.

Mediterranean cod

Serves 4

225 calories per serving

Takes 10 minutes to prepare,
30–35 minutes to cook

2 x 400 g cans artichokes,
drained and rinsed

1 kg (2 lb 4 oz) courgettes,
halved lengthways and cut
into thick pieces

400 g (14 oz) cherry or baby
plum tomatoes, halved

a small bunch of fresh thyme,
chopped

2 tablespoons capers, drained
and rinsed

calorie controlled cooking
spray

4 x 150 g (5½ oz) skinless cod
fillets

grated zest and juice of a
lemon

100 ml (3½ fl oz) vegetable
stock

salt and freshly ground black
pepper

a small bunch of fresh parsley,
chopped, to serve

*Baked in the oven, this dish is quick and simple to make,
yet its robust flavours and beautiful colours make it
impressive enough to serve to guests.*

1 Preheat the oven to Gas Mark 7/220°C/fan oven 200°C.
Toss together the artichokes, courgettes, tomatoes, thyme
and capers in a large ovenproof dish or non stick roasting tin.
Season and spray with the cooking spray.

2 Roast for 15 minutes, until the vegetables begin to brown at
the edges. Lay the cod fillets on top of the vegetable mixture
and pour over the lemon juice and vegetable stock. Scatter
with the lemon zest. Roast for a further 15–20 minutes, or until
the cod is just cooked through.

3 Remove from the oven and scatter with the parsley to serve.

Spicy prawns

Serves 4
180 calories per serving
Takes 15 minutes

calorie controlled cooking
   spray
1 onion, sliced finely
2 garlic cloves, sliced
125 ml (4 fl oz) dry white wine
1 tablespoon paprika
a generous pinch of ground
   mace
1–2 red chillies, de-seeded
   and diced finely
300 g (10½ oz) raw peeled
   tiger prawns, defrosted if
   frozen
200 g (7 oz) half fat crème
   fraîche
2 tablespoons chopped fresh
   coriander
salt and freshly ground black
   pepper

Spice up your meals with this fiery seafood sauce.

1 Heat a wide non stick saucepan and spray with the cooking spray. Add the onion and garlic and cook for 3–4 minutes until beginning to soften. Pour in the wine and allow it to bubble for 1 minute.

2 Add the paprika, mace, chillies and prawns. Cook for 1 minute. Stir in the crème fraîche and cook for 2–3 minutes until the prawns are cooked. Stir in the coriander, season and serve immediately.

Sweet and sour fish curry

Serves 2
260 calories per serving
Takes 45 minutes
❄

calorie controlled cooking
  spray
1 small red onion, cubed
75 g (2¾ oz) carrots, peeled
  and diced finely
1 garlic clove, crushed
1 tablespoon korma curry
  powder
150 g (5½ oz) courgettes,
  diced
400 g can chopped tomatoes
150 ml (5 fl oz) fish stock
1 tablespoon lemon juice
100 g (3½ oz) baby corn,
  halved
100 g (3½ oz) canned
  pineapple chunks in natural
  juice, drained
275 g (9½ oz) skinless
  haddock fillet, cubed
2 tablespoons chopped fresh
  coriander, to serve

*This is quite a mild curry, with the pineapple adding
sweetness to the sauce.*

1 Heat a large non stick pan and spray it with the cooking
spray. Add the onion, carrots, garlic and curry powder with
2 tablespoons of water and cook, stirring, over a low heat for
5 minutes, until the vegetables have softened.

2 Add the courgettes, tomatoes, fish stock and lemon juice
to the pan and bring to the boil. Reduce the heat and simmer,
uncovered, for 15 minutes.

3 Mix in the baby corn, pineapple and haddock, stir well and
cook for a further 10 minutes.

4 Sprinkle with the coriander just before serving.

Italian seafood stew

Serves 4

216 calories per serving

Takes 15 minutes to prepare,
35 minutes to cook

**calorie controlled cooking
spray**

1 onion, chopped finely

2 celery sticks, sliced finely

**2 carrots, peeled and sliced
thickly**

100 g (3½ oz) dried macaroni

600 ml (20 fl oz) fish stock

2 bay leaves

**1 large preserved lemon from
a jar, drained and sliced**

400 g can chopped tomatoes

**400 g (14 oz) frozen mixed
seafood**

**salt and freshly ground black
pepper**

**1 tablespoon chopped fresh
dill, to garnish**

This would also make a great starter for eight.

1 Heat a large, lidded, non stick saucepan and spray with the cooking spray. Cook the onion, celery and carrots for 5–8 minutes until beginning to soften but not brown.

2 Stir in the pasta, fish stock, bay leaves, lemon slices and tomatoes. Bring to the boil, cover and simmer gently for 30 minutes until the pasta is cooked.

3 Stir in the seafood and cook for 5 minutes more. Check the seasoning, remove the bay leaves and serve in warmed bowls sprinkled with the dill.

Moules provençales

Serves 4
100 calories per serving
Takes 20 minutes

calorie controlled cooking
   spray
2 garlic cloves, chopped finely
1 onion, chopped finely
150 ml (5 fl oz) vegetable or
   fish stock
400 g can chopped tomatoes
a bunch of fresh basil or
   thyme, chopped
1 kg (2 lb 4 oz) mussels,
   prepared (see Tip)
salt and freshly ground black
   pepper

A very quick and simple recipe for one of the British Isles' most common and delectable shellfish. Serve with a 50 g (1¾ oz) slice of crusty fresh bread to mop up the juices.

1 Heat a large, lidded, non stick saucepan and spray with the cooking spray. Sauté the garlic and onion for 5 minutes until soft, adding a splash of water if necessary to prevent them from sticking.

2 Add the stock, tomatoes, herbs and seasoning and cook briskly for 5 minutes. Add the mussels, cover and continue to cook for another 5 minutes, shaking the pan vigorously a few times.

3 When you remove the lid the mussels should have fully opened. Discard any that have not. Spoon into serving bowls and serve.

Tip... To prepare mussels, scrub off any dirt and remove any barnacles. Remove the beard, if any, that sticks out between the shells. Discard any mussels that are already open or have a cracked shell.

Tiger prawn curry

Serves 4
155 calories per serving
Takes 45 minutes

calorie controlled cooking
  spray
1 teaspoon black mustard
  seeds
400 g can chopped tomatoes
500 g (1 lb 2 oz) raw peeled
  tiger prawns, defrosted if
  frozen
100 g (3½ oz) low fat natural
  yogurt
a small bunch of fresh
  coriander, chopped
salt and freshly ground black
  pepper

For the curry paste
1 onion, chopped
3 garlic cloves, crushed
2 red or green chillies,
  de-seeded and chopped
2 cm (¾ inch) fresh root
  ginger, chopped roughly
4 teaspoons paprika
1 teaspoon garam masala
1 teaspoon ground coriander
½ teaspoon turmeric
juice of ½ a lemon

*Making your own curry paste is not as difficult as you
might think.*

1 First make the curry paste by placing all the ingredients
in a food processor with 1 tablespoon of water and blending
until smooth.

2 Heat a large non stick frying pan, spray with the cooking
spray and fry the mustard seeds. When they begin to pop, add
the home-made curry paste and fry for 4–5 minutes.

3 Add 250 ml (9 fl oz) of water and stir in. Stir in the tomatoes
and cook for a further 5 minutes. Add the prawns and simmer
gently for 3–4 minutes, until the prawns are just firm and pink.
Check the seasoning and remove from the heat.

4 When cooled a little, gently fold in the yogurt and coriander
and serve.

Variation... The curry paste used in this recipe could also
be used with chicken, turkey or other fish.

Pizza topped fish fillets

Serves 4

156 calories per serving

Takes 5 minutes to prepare,
10 minutes to cook

**4 x 125 g (4½ oz) chunky
haddock or cod loins**

**calorie controlled cooking
spray**

4 ripe tomatoes, sliced thickly

**12 stoned black olives in
brine, drained and sliced**

**2 tablespoons fresh basil,
shredded**

**60 g (2 oz) mozzarella light,
diced**

**salt and freshly ground black
pepper**

This is a fantastic way to bake fish fillets.

1 Preheat the oven to Gas Mark 5/190°C/fan oven 170°C.

2 Place the pieces of fish on a non stick baking tray that has been lightly sprayed with the cooking spray. Season the fish fillets and lay the tomato slices on top.

3 Scatter the olives, basil and mozzarella over and bake for 10 minutes until the cheese has melted and the fish flakes easily.

Simply vegetarian

Root and orange soup

Serves 6

75 calories per serving

Takes 15 minutes to prepare,
  20 minutes to cook

Ⓥ

❄

**500 g (1 lb 2 oz) carrots,
  peeled and diced**

**1 small swede, peeled and
  diced**

2 red onions, chopped

1 garlic clove, crushed

**1½ litres (2¾ pints) hot
  vegetable stock**

1 tablespoon tomato purée

1 tablespoon balsamic vinegar

**finely grated zest and juice of
  an orange**

**1 tablespoon chopped fresh
  parsley or chives, plus extra
  to garnish**

**salt and freshly ground black
  pepper**

This delicious soup is full of flavour and healthy too.

1 Put the carrots, swede, onions and garlic into a large saucepan. Add the stock, tomato purée and balsamic vinegar and stir well. Bring up to the boil, reduce the heat to low and simmer gently for 15–20 minutes, until the vegetables are tender.

2 Leave the soup chunky or whizz in a blender or using a hand blender until smooth. Stir in the orange zest and juice with the parsley or chives and check the seasoning.

3 Ladle the soup into warmed bowls and garnish with the extra parsley or chives.

Variations... For a special garnish, top each portion with 1 tablespoon low fat natural yogurt and a little grated orange zest, as well as the extra parsley or chives.

Ring the changes with lemon zest and juice instead of orange, and change the vegetables according to their availability – for instance, use spring onions or shallots instead of red onions.

Indian omelette

Serves 1
225 calories
Takes 10 minutes
Ⓥ

calorie controlled cooking spray
½ small onion, sliced thinly
½ red or green chilli, de-seeded and diced
2 eggs
a pinch of ground cumin
1 tomato, diced
2 heaped tablespoons chopped fresh coriander
salt and freshly ground black pepper

This is a great way to jazz up an omelette.

1 Heat a non stick frying pan until hot and spray with the cooking spray. Fry the onion and chilli for 4–5 minutes, adding a splash of water if necessary to prevent them from sticking.

2 Beat the eggs with 1 tablespoon of water, the cumin and seasoning. Stir in the tomato and coriander and pour this mixture into the frying pan.

3 Cook over a medium heat until the omelette is golden underneath and just set on top. Turn out on to a warmed plate.

Variation... Try something a little different by serving the omelette rolled up inside a medium chapati or soft flour tortilla.

Moroccan Quorn mince

Serves 4
195 calories per serving
Takes 25 minutes

Warming spices and chick peas give vegetarian mince a delicious Moroccan flavour.

1 Heat a lidded flameproof casserole dish on the hob and spray with the cooking spray. Add the onion and cook for 3 minutes and then add the spices, Quorn mince and flour and cook for 1 minute, stirring.

2 Add the stock, lemon zest, lemon juice and chick peas. Bring to the boil, cover and simmer for 12 minutes. Add the coriander before serving.

Variation... For a non vegetarian version, try replacing the Quorn mince with the same quantity of lean minced lamb and following the same instructions.

calorie controlled cooking spray
1 red onion, chopped
½ teaspoon ground cinnamon
1 teaspoon ground cumin
350 g (12 oz) Quorn mince
1 tablespoon plain white flour
450 ml (16 fl oz) hot vegetable stock
grated zest and juice of ½ a lemon
410 g can chick peas, drained and rinsed
4 heaped tablespoons roughly chopped fresh coriander

Vegetable dhal

Serves 4
195 calories per serving
Takes 20 minutes

Y
❄

100 g (3½ oz) dried red lentils
½ a kettleful of boiling water
calorie controlled cooking
    spray
1 small onion, chopped finely
1 courgette, cut into chunks
150 g (5½ oz) baby button
    mushrooms
1 carrot, peeled and grated
2 teaspoons black mustard
    seeds
175 g (6 oz) frozen chopped
    spinach
2 tablespoons medium curry
    powder
30 g (1¼ oz) creamed coconut,
    crumbled
75 g (2¾ oz) paneer cheese,
    cubed
salt and freshly ground black
    pepper

Scoop up the delicious dhal with a 45 g (1½ oz) fat free chapati per person.

1 Put the lentils into a large bowl and cover with the boiling water. Microwave on high for 5 minutes and then drain and rinse in cold water.

2 Meanwhile, heat a wide, lidded, non stick saucepan and spray with the cooking spray. Cook the onion, courgette and mushrooms for 3 minutes until softened.

3 Add the carrot, mustard seeds, frozen spinach, cooked lentils, curry powder and 5 tablespoons of cool water. Cover and cook over a low heat for 5–7 minutes, stirring from time to time.

4 Stir in the creamed coconut and paneer cheese and cook for a further 5 minutes until heated through. Season to taste and serve immediately.

Variation... You could use 75 g (2¾ oz) diced hard goat's cheese instead of the paneer.

Winter vegetable casserole with spicy dumplings

Serves 4
306 calories per serving
Takes 30 minutes to prepare, 40 minutes to cook ⊘

This recipe is great for warming you up on those cold winter days. Try exchanging some of the vegetables for your own favourites to give it that personal touch.

For the dumplings
90 g (3¼ oz) self raising flour
1 teaspoon ground coriander
1 teaspoon cumin seeds
2 tablespoons low fat spread

For the casserole
2 teaspoons vegetable oil
90 g (3¼ oz) shallots or small onions, halved
1 leek, sliced

1 large carrot, peeled and sliced
225 g (8 oz) parsnips, peeled and chopped
2 celery sticks, chopped
1.2 litres (2 pints) vegetable stock
25 g (1 oz) dried pearl barley or bulgur wheat
400 g can chick peas, drained and rinsed
175 g (6 oz) cauliflower, broken into florets
salt and freshly ground black pepper
a handful of fresh parsley or coriander, to garnish (optional)

1 For the dumplings, sift the flour into a large bowl and then mix in the ground coriander and cumin seeds. Rub in the low fat spread until the mixture resembles fine breadcrumbs. Add enough cold water to make a soft, but not sticky, dough, form into eight dumplings, cover and set aside.

2 Heat the oil in a large lidded saucepan and sauté the shallots or onions, leek, carrot, parsnips and celery for 5 minutes, without browning them.

continues overleaf ▶

3 Add the stock, pearl barley or bulgur wheat and chick peas to the saucepan. Bring to the boil, reduce the heat, cover and simmer for 20 minutes.

4 Add the cauliflower and dumplings to the saucepan. Cover and simmer for 20 minutes or until the dumplings are cooked – they should be light and fluffy.

5 Season the casserole to taste. Serve, garnished with the parsley or coriander, if using, allowing two dumplings per person.

Mushroom and leek crumble

Serves 2

325 calories per serving

Takes 15 minutes to prepare,
  30 minutes to cook

Ⓥ

**calorie controlled cooking
  spray**

**6 open mushrooms, halved
  and sliced thickly**

2 leeks, sliced thickly

1 garlic clove, crushed

**400 g can chopped tomatoes
  with herbs**

1 tablespoon tomato purée

½ teaspoon dried mixed herbs

**salt and freshly ground black
  pepper**

For the crumble

50 g (1¾ oz) plain white flour

25 g (1 oz) porridge oats

**½ teaspoon English mustard
  powder**

15 g (½ oz) low fat spread

**50 g (1¾ oz) half fat Cheddar
  cheese**

*Here's another supper to enjoy. Mushrooms and leeks
topped with a golden crumble topping.*

1 Preheat the oven to Gas Mark 5/190°C/fan oven 170°C.
Spray a large, lidded, flameproof casserole dish with the
cooking spray, add the mushrooms and leeks and stir-fry for
5 minutes, or until softened. Add the garlic and cook for a
further minute or two.

2 Stir in the tomatoes, tomato purée and herbs. Season, cover
and simmer for 10 minutes.

3 To make the crumble, place the flour, oats, mustard powder
and low fat spread in a bowl and rub together until the mixture
becomes crumbly. Mix in the cheese and season lightly.

4 Remove the mushroom and leek mixture from the heat and
cover with the crumble. Cook in the oven for 30 minutes or
until the topping is golden and crisp.

Sicilian aubergines

Serves 4

150 calories per serving

Takes 20 minutes to prepare + cooling, 35 minutes to cook

Ⓥ

2 tablespoons pine nut kernels

calorie controlled cooking spray

1 onion, sliced finely

500 g (1 lb 2 oz) aubergines, diced

1 teaspoon dried oregano or 1 tablespoon chopped fresh oregano

400 g can chopped tomatoes

1 tablespoon clear honey

50 g (1¾ oz) stoned green or black olives in brine, rinsed and chopped roughly

3 tablespoons capers, rinsed

1 tablespoon red wine vinegar

salt and freshly ground black pepper

Here is a delicious version of a well-known dish – caponata.

1 Toast the pine nut kernels in a large, dry, lidded, non stick frying pan until golden brown. Remove and set aside.

2 Spray the frying pan with the cooking spray and fry the onion for about 4 minutes until soft. Add the aubergines and oregano and cook, turning frequently, for 5 minutes.

3 Add all the remaining ingredients, except the pine nut kernels. Cover and simmer for 35 minutes.

4 Taste and adjust the seasoning, adding more vinegar or honey if necessary to achieve a good sweet and sour balance.

5 For the best flavour, allow the caponata to cool to room temperature and then scatter over the pine nut kernels just before serving.

Tip... Caponata tastes even better if it is left overnight in the fridge and then brought back to room temperature again before serving.

Risotto of summer vegetables

Serves 4
279 calories per serving
Takes 55 minutes
Ⓥ

calorie controlled cooking
spray
4 large spring onions, chopped
250 g (9 oz) dried risotto rice
**850 ml (1½ pints) hot
vegetable stock**
1 courgette, sliced thinly
**2 small carrots, peeled and cut
into matchsticks**
**125 g (4½ oz) fine asparagus,
halved if very long**
**¼ kettleful of boiling water
(optional)**
**100 g (3½ oz) frozen peas,
defrosted**
**75 g (2¾ oz) low fat soft
cheese**
**6 fresh chives, snipped, to
garnish**

*Use whatever vegetables are in season for this simple,
fresh risotto.*

1 Heat a wok or large non stick frying pan and spray it with
the cooking spray. Gently fry the spring onions for 2 minutes.
Add the rice and stir for a further 2 minutes, until the rice
becomes opaque.

2 Keeping the heat fairly low, add a couple of ladles of stock
to the rice. Stir until the liquid is absorbed. The temperature
will be right when you can just see a few bubbles rising to the
surface, but not a vigorous boil.

3 Keep adding the stock, a couple of ladles at a time,
always allowing it to be absorbed before adding more. After
10 minutes (you will have used about half the stock), add the
courgette, carrots and asparagus. Stir and continue adding the
stock as before. After 25–30 minutes, the rice should be tender
with a rich, creamy consistency. If you run out of stock, use a
little boiling water.

4 Add the peas and stir them in to heat through. Finally stir
in the soft cheese and serve in warm bowls with the chives
sprinkled on top.

Mixed bean chilli

Serves 4

200 calories per serving

Takes 20 minutes to prepare,
30 minutes to cook

Ⓥ

❄

1 tablespoon olive oil

1 onion, sliced

2 garlic cloves, crushed

175 g (6 oz) carrots, peeled
and diced

1 red pepper, de-seeded and
diced

1 green pepper, de-seeded and
diced

150 g (5½ oz) button
mushrooms, quartered

1 cooking apple, peeled, cored
and grated

1 tablespoon mild chilli
powder

225 g can chopped tomatoes

400 g can mixed beans in
chilli sauce

2 tablespoons chopped fresh
parsley, to garnish

*A handy dish to make up and keep in individual portions in
the freezer. Try it with a 50 g (1¾ oz) chunk of crusty bread
per person.*

1 Heat the olive oil in a large, lidded, non stick pan and
cook the onion, garlic, carrots, peppers and mushrooms for
5 minutes.

2 Stir in the grated apple and chilli powder and cook for a
further 2 minutes.

3 Stir in the tomatoes and mixed beans. Cover and simmer for
30 minutes. Sprinkle over the chopped parsley and serve hot.

Bolognese bake

Serves 4

378 calories per serving

Takes 10 minutes to prepare,
40–45 minutes to cook

Ⓥ

½ onion, grated

2 garlic cloves, crushed

350 g packet vegetarian mince

400 g can chopped tomatoes

1 tablespoon dried oregano

1 tablespoon tomato purée

150 ml (5 fl oz) vegetable
stock

125 g (4½ oz) fresh fusilli
pasta

300 g (10½ oz) low fat soft
cheese with garlic and herbs

2 egg yolks

salt and freshly ground black
pepper

*This has to be the world's easiest adaptation of the
favourite spaghetti bolognese.*

1 Preheat the oven to Gas Mark 4/180°C/fan oven 160°C. In
a large bowl, mix together the onion, garlic, mince, tomatoes,
oregano and tomato purée. Stir through the stock and pasta
and then season. Spoon into a 1½ litre (2¾ pint) ovenproof
dish.

2 Mix together the soft cheese and egg yolks and season.
Spread over the top of the pasta and mince. Bake in the oven
for 40–45 minutes until golden and bubbling.

Roasted Mediterranean vegetables

Serves 4

265 calories per serving

Takes 10 minutes to prepare,
40–45 minutes to cook

Ⓥ

2 tablespoons olive oil

175 g (6 oz) baby new
potatoes, scrubbed and
halved

3 red onions, each cut into
8 wedges

4 small parsnips, peeled and
quartered lengthways

1 large butternut squash,
peeled, de-seeded and cut
into chunks

2 large courgettes, sliced

1 red pepper, de-seeded and
cut into chunks

1 yellow pepper, de-seeded
and cut into chunks

½ teaspoon cumin seeds
(optional)

a few fresh thyme and
rosemary sprigs

16 cherry tomatoes

salt and freshly ground black
pepper

a few fresh basil leaves, to
garnish

*These colourful vegetables taste fantastic; the roasting
concentrates their flavours beautifully.*

1 Preheat the oven to Gas Mark 6/200°C/fan oven 180°C.

2 Pour the olive oil into a non stick roasting tin and add the
potatoes, onions, parsnips, squash, courgettes and peppers.
Season, add the cumin seeds, if using, and then toss together
so that all the vegetables are coated with the oil. Add the thyme
and rosemary sprigs.

3 Roast for 30 minutes. Add the tomatoes and roast for
another 10–15 minutes, or until the vegetables are tender.
Serve garnished with the basil leaves.

Variations... These roasted vegetables taste fantastic
served with 1 tablespoon mango chutney and 1 tablespoon
half fat crème fraîche per person.

If you can't find a butternut squash, use 2 aubergines
instead, cut into chunks.

The cumin seeds add a wonderful aroma and flavour,
though you could use 2 teaspoons of dried oregano as an
alternative.

Sweet potato and pea tagine

Serves 4
285 calories per serving
Takes 15 minutes to prepare,
  25 minutes to cook

Ⓥ
❄ (for up to 1 month)

2 tablespoons lemon juice
2 teaspoons clear honey
1 teaspoon ground cinnamon
½ teaspoon chilli powder
calorie controlled cooking
  spray
1 large onion, sliced
2 garlic cloves, sliced
750 g (1 lb 10 oz) sweet
  potato, peeled and cut into
  bite size pieces
100 g (3½ oz) frozen peas
2 medium pitta breads, to
  serve

A delicious North African dish that is normally cooked in a traditional shallow earthenware cooking pot called a tagine.

1 In a small bowl or jug, mix together 1 tablespoon of the lemon juice with the honey, cinnamon and chilli powder. Set aside.

2 Heat a large non stick pan and spray with the cooking spray. Add the onion and garlic and cook for 4–5 minutes, until starting to soften. Add the sweet potato and the honey and lemon juice mixture and stir really well.

3 Pour in the remaining lemon juice and 200 ml (7 fl oz) of water. Bring to the boil and simmer for 15 minutes.

4 Add the peas and bring back to a simmer for another 10 minutes, or until the sweet potato is tender.

5 Serve with the pitta bread cut into slices, for dipping in the sauce.

Variation... Substitute butternut squash for the sweet potato if you wish.

Stir-fried broccoli and tofu

Serves 2
205 calories per serving
Takes 15 minutes
Ⓥ

calorie controlled cooking
  spray
2 garlic cloves, sliced finely
2.5 cm (1 inch) fresh root
  ginger, chopped finely
150 g (5½ oz) smoked tofu
  pieces
1 large carrot, peeled and cut
  into matchsticks
1 head broccoli, cut into
  florets and the stem diced
4 tablespoons soy sauce
juice of ½ a lemon
150 ml (5 fl oz) vegetable
  stock
a small bunch of fresh
  coriander, chopped

*For this dish you need smoked tofu available from the
chiller section of larger supermarkets or from health or
Asian food shops.*

1 Heat a wok or large non stick frying pan and spray with the
cooking spray. Stir-fry the garlic and ginger for a few moments
until they turn golden.

2 Add the tofu and vegetables and stir-fry them together. Add
the soy sauce, lemon juice and stock and mix together.

3 Stir-fry for a further 2–4 minutes, until most of the liquid has
evaporated and the vegetables are al dente, and then serve
scattered with the coriander.

Tip... Soy sauce is an essential condiment, particularly
if you like Oriental foods. You can use it to colour and
flavour marinades, dips and sauces. Light soy sauce has a
delicate, salty flavour that goes well with white meats and
seafood. Use dark soy sauce (which is thicker, richer but
less salty) with meats or in stews.

Quorn satay noodles

Serves 1
559 calories
Takes 15 minutes
Ⓥ

Enjoy your favourite stir-fry veggies in this dish.

calorie controlled cooking
  spray
½ onion, sliced
52 g frozen Quorn fillet
15 g (½ oz) fresh root ginger,
  diced finely
250 ml (9 fl oz) hot vegetable
  stock
½ x 350 g packet mixed
  stir-fry vegetables
50 g (1¾ oz) dried medium
  egg noodles
40 g (1½ oz) reduced fat
  smooth peanut butter
a pinch of dried chilli flakes
50 g (1¾ oz) frozen peas
lime wedges, to serve

1 Heat a wide, lidded, non stick saucepan and spray with the cooking spray. Cook the onion, Quorn and ginger for 3–4 minutes until everything is starting to soften. Remove the Quorn fillet and cut into pieces.

2 Return the Quorn pieces to the pan along with the stock, mixed vegetables and noodles. Cover and cook for 5 minutes, stirring occasionally.

3 Add the peanut butter, chilli flakes and peas. Cover and gently heat for 3 minutes, stirring occasionally until the vegetables are tender and the sauce has thickened. Serve immediately in a warmed bowl, with lime wedges to squeeze over.

Goat's cheese and lentil stuffed peppers

Serves 2
356 calories per serving
Takes 25 minutes
Ⓥ

400 g can Puy lentils, drained
  and rinsed

½ red onion, diced finely

1 tablespoon fresh rosemary
  leaves

2 tablespoons reduced fat
  pesto

grated zest and juice of a
  small lemon

2 red peppers, halved and
  de-seeded

calorie controlled cooking
  spray

50 g (1¾ oz) goat's cheese
  with rind, cut into four slices

salt and freshly ground black
  pepper

Puy lentils are French dark green lentils with a uniquely peppery flavour. You'll find them in most supermarkets beside the tinned pulses.

1 Preheat the oven to Gas Mark 6/200°C/fan oven 180°C. Mix the lentils, onion, rosemary, pesto, lemon zest, lemon juice and seasoning in a bowl.

2 Place the pepper halves on a non stick baking tray, cut side up, and fill them equally with the lentil mixture. Spray with the cooking spray and bake in the oven for 15 minutes.

3 Remove the peppers from the oven and top each with a slice of goat's cheese. Season and return to the oven. Bake for 5 minutes until just melted. Serve immediately.

Tip... This also makes a great starter for four.

Chick pea coconut stew

Serves 4
165 calories per serving
Takes 25 minutes
Ⓥ

calorie controlled cooking
  spray
4 shallots, sliced finely
1 lemongrass stalk, outer
  leaves removed and sliced
  finely
1 small red chilli, de-seeded
  and diced finely
120 g (4½ oz) shiitake
  mushrooms, sliced
150 g (5½ oz) tenderstem
  broccoli, halved
2 teaspoons cornflour
410 g can chick peas, drained
  and rinsed
150 g (5½ oz) Savoy cabbage,
  cored and shredded
600 ml (20 fl oz) vegetable
  stock
½ x 400 ml can reduced fat
  coconut milk

Enjoy this with a 50 g (1¾ oz) bread roll per person, to mop up the juices.

1 Heat a large non stick saucepan and spray with the cooking spray. Cook the shallots, lemongrass and chilli for 2 minutes. Spray the pan again and stir in the mushrooms and broccoli. Cook for 3 minutes.

2 Stir in the cornflour, chick peas and cabbage. Gradually stir in the vegetable stock and coconut milk. Bring to a simmer and bubble for 10 minutes until thickened and tender. Spoon into warmed bowls and serve immediately.

Potato parcels

Serves 4

90 calories per serving

Takes 20 minutes to prepare,
30 minutes to cook

Ⓥ
❄

450 g (1 lb) small new
potatoes, scrubbed and
sliced

1 red onion, sliced

1 garlic clove, sliced very
thinly

4 fresh thyme sprigs

calorie controlled cooking
spray

125 ml (4 fl oz) vegetable
stock

salt and freshly ground black
pepper

*This is an interesting way to cook potatoes as it keeps
all their flavour in and there's also no pan to clear up
afterwards.*

1 Preheat the oven to Gas Mark 5/190°C/fan oven 170°C.

2 Lay four sheets of non stick baking parchment, each about
30 cm (12 inches) square, on a flat work surface.

3 Divide the potato and onion slices between the paper
sheets. Top each potato and onion pile with a little garlic, a
thyme sprig and some seasoning. Spray each mound with
a little cooking spray.

4 Gather together the edges of each sheet, to enclose the
potatoes, but do not seal them up yet. Pour a little stock
into each parcel and then fold the paper over a few times to
completely enclose the mixture.

5 Place the parcels on a baking tray and bake for
30 minutes.

Tip... Make sure you wrap up the baking parchment tightly
as the steam that forms in the parcels cooks the potatoes,
and be very careful as you open each parcel as steam will
escape and may burn you.

Delicious desserts

Pineapple tarte tatin

Serves 8
130 calories per serving
Takes 15 minutes to prepare
  + 10 minutes cooling,
  25 minutes to bake

Ⓥ
❋

1 teaspoon plain white flour,
  for rolling
150 g (5½ oz) ready-made puff
  pastry, defrosted if frozen
227 g can pineapple rings in
  natural juice, drained and
  halved
15 g (½ oz) low fat spread,
  melted
2 tablespoons demerara sugar

A tarte tatin is cooked upside down, with the pastry on the top, and then turned over to serve.

1 Preheat the oven to Gas Mark 5/190°C/fan oven 170°C.

2 Lightly dust a work surface with the flour and roll out the puff pastry to make a 23 cm (9 inch) circle.

3 Arrange the pineapple rings in a 20 cm (8 inch), heavy based, ovenproof frying pan with a metal handle, or a round cake tin. Drizzle the melted low fat spread over the pineapple and then sprinkle over the sugar. Lay the pastry circle over the top of the fruit and tuck in the edges.

4 Bake the tart in the oven for 25 minutes. Remove from the oven and allow it to cool in the pan or tin for 10 minutes. When ready to serve, place a plate on top and turn the pan or tin upside down so that the tart drops on to the plate. Serve the tart warm or cold, sliced into wedges.

Tip... Make sure you use a good quality non stick pan or tin for this very simple yet effective dessert.

Variation... Canned peach halves or apricots make a good alternative to the pineapple in this recipe.

Apple bread pudding

Serves 4

181 calories per serving

Takes 5 minutes to prepare, 25 minutes to cook

Ⓥ

calorie controlled cooking spray

200 g (7 oz) low fat vanilla yogurt

1 egg, beaten

½ teaspoon mixed spice

100 g (3½ oz) apple sauce

25 g (1 oz) light brown soft sugar

100 g (3½ oz) crustless white or wholemeal bread, diced

1 apple, cored and diced

This is best made with slightly stale bread, so it's ideal for using up the end of a loaf in the bread bin. Instead of buying apple sauce, you can make it by chopping an apple, cooking it in a little water and then mashing it.

1 Preheat the oven to Gas Mark 4/180°C/fan oven 160°C. Spray an ovenproof baking dish with the cooking spray.

2 Reserve half the yogurt to serve. In a bowl, mix the remaining yogurt together with the beaten egg, mixed spice, apple sauce and sugar.

3 Stir the bread into the mixture, mixing well to coat, and then stir in the apple. Spoon into the baking dish and bake in the oven for 25 minutes until firm, with a golden brown crispy top.

4 Serve with the reserved vanilla yogurt drizzled over the hot pudding.

Cinnamon peach compote

Serves 4
59 calories per serving
Takes 15 minutes + cooling
Ⓥ

4 peaches, stoned and cut into quarters
1 lemongrass stalk, bruised
2 cm (¾ inch) fresh root ginger, sliced
1 cinnamon stick
1 teaspoon artificial sweetener

This is a lovely flavoured dessert.

1 Place all the ingredients in a pan and just cover with water.

2 Bring to the boil and simmer for 8–10 minutes depending on the ripeness of the fruit. Leave to cool in the syrup and then serve.

Fired strawberries

Serves 4
40 calories per serving
Takes 15 minutes
Ⓥ

400 g (14 oz) strawberries, hulled
grated zest and juice of a large orange
2 teaspoons ground cinnamon

These strawberries are great served with low fat ice cream.

1 Preheat the grill to high, place a griddle pan over a high heat or prepare your barbecue.

2 Place the strawberries in the centre of a 30 x 30 cm (12 x 12 inch) foil square and sprinkle over the orange zest, orange juice and cinnamon.

3 Fold up the foil to make a sealed parcel. Place under the grill or on the barbecue or griddle pan for 10 minutes, until the strawberries are soft and the juice has turned to syrup.

4 Unfold the parcel and spoon on to serving plates immediately.

Variation... Try other soft fruit such as raspberries or blackberries, or try tropical or stone fruits like mangos, papaya, pineapple, plums or peaches.

Mint and raspberry jellies

Serves 4

17 calories per serving

Takes 15 minutes + 1 hour chilling

10 fresh mint leaves, torn

300 ml (10 fl oz) boiling water

1 sachet raspberry sugar free jelly

125 g (4½ oz) raspberries, defrosted if frozen

These make a lovely, refreshing summer pudding and are particularly good for alfresco dining.

1 Place the mint leaves in a jug and pour over the boiling water. Leave to infuse for 5 minutes.

2 Add the jelly to the jug and stir to dissolve. If it doesn't dissolve fully, microwave for a few seconds and stir again.

3 Reserve four raspberries and roughly crush the rest with a fork. Stir the crushed raspberries into the jelly and top up with cold water to make 600 ml (20 fl oz). Divide between four glasses. Cool and chill in the fridge for 1 hour until set.

4 Serve decorated with the reserved raspberries.

Variation... Try this recipe using orange sugar free jelly and fresh blueberries.

Slow roasted plums

Serves 4
46 calories per serving
Takes 10 minutes to prepare,
1½ hours to cook
Ⓥ

6 slightly under-ripe plums,
  halved and stoned
2 tablespoons balsamic
  vinegar
2 teaspoons vanilla extract
2 fresh lemon thyme sprigs,
  leaves only

*Cooking at a low temperature for a long time brings out
the natural sugars in the plums. Serve with 1 tablespoon of
virtually fat free plain fromage frais per person.*

1 Preheat the oven to Gas Mark 2/150°C/fan oven 130°C. Put
the plum halves into a small ovenproof dish and bake in the
oven for 1 hour.

2 Meanwhile, mix together the balsamic vinegar, vanilla
extract, lemon thyme and 4 tablespoons of cold water
in a bowl. Pour over the plums and continue to cook for
30 minutes until the juices have reduced to a syrup. Enjoy
hot or cold.

Orange and pumpkin mousses

Serves 4

85 calories per serving

Takes 20 minutes to prepare + 30 minutes chilling + cooling

Ⓥ

110 g (4 oz) pumpkin or butternut squash, peeled, de-seeded and chopped

1 cinnamon stick, broken in half

2 oranges, with finely grated zest from 1

2 tablespoons artificial sweetener

400 g (14 oz) virtually fat free plain fromage frais

Pumpkin is naturally sweet and great at taking on other flavours such as spices.

1 Place the pumpkin or squash in a lidded pan with the cinnamon stick and 4 tablespoons of water. Bring to the boil, cover and simmer for 10 minutes until soft. Remove the cinnamon stick, drain thoroughly and mash.

2 Cut the skin from both the oranges and segment, collecting any juices from the segments.

3 Stir the orange zest and sweetener into the mashed pumpkin with any juices from the oranges. Set aside to cool completely.

4 Once cool, fold in the fromage frais and spoon into serving glasses. Chill for 30 minutes before serving. Decorate with the orange segments.

Variation... If you have ground cinnamon to hand, flavour the cooked and mashed pumpkin with 1 teaspoon instead of cooking it with the cinnamon stick.

Cherry brûlée

Serves 2
175 calories per serving
Takes 10 minutes
Ⓥ

150 g (5½ oz) cherries, stoned
125 g (4½ oz) Quark
100 g (3½ oz) virtually fat free
  plain fromage frais
½ teaspoon vanilla extract
50 g (1¾ oz) demerara sugar

Quark is a very low fat soft cheese that is ideal for making desserts.

1 Preheat the grill to its highest setting.

2 Place the cherries in the bases of two ramekins. Whisk the Quark and fromage frais together with the vanilla extract until smooth. Spoon on top of the fruit and level the surface.

3 Sprinkle the demerara sugar evenly over the top and mist lightly with water (this helps the sugar to dissolve quickly under the grill). Pop under the hot grill and cook for 2–3 minutes until the sugar has melted and begun to caramelise.

4 Allow the brûlées to cool, and the caramel to harden, for a couple of minutes before eating.

Tip... You can use an olive stoner to stone cherries if you have one but, if not, place the cherries on a chopping board and lightly crush with a rolling pin or filled can to release the stones.

Cherry and almond omelette

Serves 6
230 calories per serving
Takes 25 minutes
Ⓥ

25 g (1 oz) butter
2 x 425 g cans stoned black cherries in syrup, drained
4 eggs, beaten
100 g (3½ oz) virtually fat free plain fromage frais
25 g (1 oz) caster sugar
25 g (1 oz) ground almonds
15 g (½ oz) flaked almonds
a dusting of icing sugar

Cherries and almonds conjure up memories of Italy with its lovely fruit orchards. This is delicious served with a scoop of low fat vanilla ice cream per person.

1 Melt the butter in a large heavy based frying pan. (The handle needs to be able to withstand the heat of the grill).

2 Heat the cherries in the butter for 3–4 minutes or until slightly softened.

3 Beat together the eggs, fromage frais, sugar and ground almonds. Pour over the cherries. Stir for 3–4 minutes and leave to lightly set for a further 5 minutes. Preheat the grill to medium.

4 Sprinkle the flaked almonds over the top and place under the grill to lightly toast the nuts. Serve warm, dusted with icing sugar.

Apricot clafouti

Serves 4

169 calories per serving

Takes 10 minutes to prepare,
20–25 minutes to cook

Ⓥ

calorie controlled cooking
spray

6 small apricots, stoned and
each sliced into 6 pieces

50 g (1¾ oz) plain white flour

50 g (1¾ oz) caster sugar

2 eggs

200 ml (7 fl oz) skimmed milk

1 teaspoon vanilla essence

Cherries are traditional in clafouti. This version uses fresh apricots instead.

1 Preheat the oven to Gas Mark 6/200°C/fan oven 180°C. Spray four shallow ovenproof dishes approximately 12 cm (4½ inches) wide with the cooking spray.

2 Place the slices from one and a half apricots (9 slices) in a circle in each one of the dishes.

3 Beat all the remaining ingredients together in a large bowl and share out the mixture between the dishes.

4 Bake in the oven for 20–25 minutes, or until golden and the tops spring back when gently pressed. Serve immediately.

Variation... If they're in season, use 300 g (10½ oz) stoned fresh cherries instead of the apricots.

Baked Alaska

Serves 4
123 calories per serving
Takes 15 minutes
Ⓥ

3 egg whites
5 tablespoons artificial sweetener
15 cm (6 inch) sponge flan case
100 g (3½ oz) frozen summer fruits, defrosted, with their juice
125 g (4½ oz) low fat vanilla ice cream
1 teaspoon caster sugar

This recipe is deceptively easy and the result looks stunning. However, you must make it just before you want to serve it.

1 Preheat the oven to Gas Mark 8/230°C/fan oven 210°C. In a clean, grease-free bowl, whisk the egg whites until they form stiff peaks. Whisk in the artificial sweetener.

2 Place the flan case on a non stick baking tray and pile the fruit, with its juice, into the very centre, leaving 5 cm (2 inches) around the edge of the flan.

3 Use a large spoon to remove the ice cream in wide strips (see Tip) and use them to cover the fruit in a dome shape. You need to leave a gap of 1 cm (½ inch) around the edge of the flan.

4 Spoon on the egg whites to form an insulating 'coat' over everything. Leave no gaps and go right to the edge of the flan. Use the back of your spoon to fluff the egg into peaks and then sprinkle with the sugar. Put immediately into the oven and cook for 3–4 minutes or until golden. Transfer it very carefully to a serving plate, take it to the table, cut into slices and serve immediately.

Tip... To weigh the ice cream, put it – still in the tub – on to the scales and then work out how much it should weigh when you have taken out 125 g.

Chocolate fondue

Serves 4
207 calories per serving
Takes 10 minutes
Ⓥ

25 g (1 oz) cocoa powder

170 g can evaporated milk

25 g (1 oz) milk chocolate,
broken into pieces

2 bananas, sliced

3 clementines or satsumas,
segmented

200 g (7 oz) strawberries,
hulled

This clever chocolate fondue sauce is rich and indulgent.

1 Place the cocoa in a non stick saucepan and gradually stir in the evaporated milk to make a smooth sauce.

2 Add the chocolate and place the pan over a medium heat. Bring to a simmer, stirring, and cook for 1 minute until thickened.

3 Pour into small individual bowls and serve with the fruit, to dip into the chocolate fondue sauce.

Baked orange and candied peel ricotta puddings

Serves 4

224 calories per serving

Takes 10 minutes to prepare,
15 minutes to bake

Ⓨ

**calorie controlled cooking
spray**

250 g (9 oz) ricotta cheese

2 eggs, beaten

½ teaspoon vanilla extract

2 tablespoons caster sugar

½ teaspoon ground cinnamon

**30 g (1¼ oz) candied peel,
chopped**

**finely grated zest of ½ an
orange, plus long zested
strips, to decorate**

*These individual puddings have a light texture and a great
orange flavour.*

1 Spray four mini pudding basins or four 150 ml (5 fl oz)
ramekins with the cooking spray and base line with non stick
baking parchment.

2 Use an electric whisk to beat together the ricotta cheese,
eggs, vanilla extract and sugar until smooth. Stir in the
cinnamon and candied peel with the orange zest. Spoon the
mixture into the basins and place in a shallow baking tin. Bake
for 15 minutes until the tops are firm but not brown.

3 To serve, run a round ended knife around the edges to
loosen and invert on to small serving plates. Decorate with the
orange zest strips. Serve warm or cold.

Tip... These puddings will keep in the fridge for up to
2 days and can be reheated in the microwave for 1 minute
or served cold.

Chocolate trifle

Serves 4
281 calories per serving
Takes 10 minutes
Ⓥ

4 **Weight Watchers Double Chocolate Muffins, sliced**
200 g (7 oz) **canned stoned black cherries in syrup, drained and syrup reserved**
2 teaspoons **orange flavoured liqueur (Grand Marnier or Cointreau)**
400 g (14 oz) **virtually fat free plain fromage frais**
grated zest of an orange

Chocolate and orange is the perfect combination in these easy trifles.

1 Divide the sliced chocolate muffins between four ramekins.

2 Top the muffins in the ramekins with the cherries. Mix the liqueur with the syrup and then pour over the cherries.

3 Stir the fromage frais and then divide between the ramekins, pouring over the cherries. Top with the orange zest and chill until ready to serve.

Quick fruit crumble

Serves 4
240 calories per serving
Takes 10 minutes to prepare,
  20 minutes to cook

This simple and satisfying dessert is assembled in no time using a can of fruit and a quickly whizzed up crumble topping – just right for a midweek pudding. Serve with low fat natural yogurt or low fat custard.

420 g can peaches in natural
  juice, drained
1 large ripe banana, sliced
  thinly
50 g (1¾ oz) low fat spread
100 g (3½ oz) plain white flour
1 tablespoon light brown soft
  sugar
2 tablespoons porridge oats
a pinch of grated nutmeg

1 Preheat the oven to Gas Mark 5/190°C/fan oven 170°C.

2 Tip the canned fruit into a medium size baking dish – chop the fruit if necessary. Mix in the banana slices.

3 Place the low fat spread, flour and sugar in a food processor and whizz until the mixture resembles fine breadcrumbs. Stir in the porridge oats. Spoon this topping over the fruit and sprinkle over the nutmeg.

4 Place the dish on a baking tray and bake in the oven for 20 minutes until the topping is lightly browned.

Variation... In spring, try 400 g (14 oz) tender, pink forced rhubarb instead of the peaches. There's no need to precook it. Just chop it and add 1 tablespoon of caster sugar.

Frozen raspberry tiramisu

Serves 8

129 calories per serving

Takes 20 minutes to prepare +
  15 minutes standing +
  4 hours freezing

Ⓥ
❄

300 g (10½ oz) low fat vanilla ice cream

4 tablespoons instant coffee granules

6 tablespoons boiling water

250 g (9 oz) fresh raspberries

20 sponge fingers (total weight 100 g/3½ oz)

3 tablespoons Belgian chocolate sauce

To decorate

2 teaspoons cocoa powder

25 g (1 oz) plain chocolate, grated

This Italian favourite will be a sure winner with the family.

1 Remove the ice cream from the freezer to soften it slightly. Meanwhile, line a 21 x 8 cm (8½ x 3¼ inch) 1.2 litre (2 pint) loaf tin tightly with enough cling film to fold over the top of the tin (brushing the tin with water first will help the cling film to stick). In a shallow bowl, mix together the coffee granules and boiling water until dissolved.

2 Fold the raspberries into the ice cream, squashing the odd one or two. Dip 10 sponge fingers into the coffee mixture, turning until coated, and then press into the base of the tin. Spread half the ice cream over the sponge fingers and drizzle with half the chocolate sauce.

3 Dip the remaining sponge fingers in the coffee mixture and arrange in a layer on top of the ice cream. Drizzle with the remaining chocolate sauce and spread over the remaining ice cream. Fold over the cling film and freeze for 4 hours until set.

4 To serve, upturn on to a serving plate and remove the cling film. Stand for 10–15 minutes and then dust the top with cocoa and grated chocolate and slice into eight.

Roasted autumn fruit salad

Serves 4

94 calories per serving

Takes 15 minutes to prepare, 40–50 minutes to cook

Ⓥ

250 g (9 oz) pears, cored and sliced

250 g (9 oz) eating apples, cored and sliced

200 g (7 oz) plums, halved and stoned

1 cinnamon stick

calorie controlled cooking spray

2–3 tablespoons artificial sweetener, to taste, plus 1 teaspoon to serve

To serve

½ teaspoon ground cinnamon

4 tablespoons 0% fat Greek yogurt

Serve this salad warm with a dollop of spiced 0% fat Greek yogurt.

1 Preheat the oven to Gas Mark 5/190°C/fan oven 170°C.

2 Place the fruit and cinnamon stick in a large non stick roasting tin and add 4 tablespoons of water. Spray generously with the cooking spray and bake for 40–50 minutes until the fruit is tender and beginning to char.

3 Remove the fruit from the oven, take out the cinnamon stick and sprinkle with 2 tablespoons of the sweetener, stirring to mix in. Taste to see if more sweetener is required. Don't worry if some of the plums are very soft as they will help to form a sauce.

4 To serve, mix the extra teaspoon of sweetener and ground cinnamon into the yogurt. Serve dolloped on top of the warm fruit.

Tip... The cooked fruit can be kept in the fridge for up to 2 days, and served either cold or warm (heat in the microwave for 30–60 seconds).

Variation... Bananas add a touch of natural sweetness to this salad, but don't need so long to cook – add 2 small bananas, peeled and sliced, for the final 15 minutes of cooking time. If adding bananas, you will not be able to store the fruit as the bananas will turn black and, although still edible, don't look very nice.

Index

Other titles in the Weight Watchers Mini Series

ISBN 978-0-85720-932-0

ISBN 978-0-85720-935-1

ISBN 978-0-85720-934-4

ISBN 978-0-85720-938-2

ISBN 978-0-85720-931-3

ISBN 978-0-85720-937-5

ISBN 978-0-85720-936-8

ISBN 978-0-85720-933-7

ISBN 978-1-47111-084-9

ISBN 978-1-47111-089-4

ISBN 978-1-47111-091-7

ISBN 978-1-47111-087-0

ISBN 978-1-47111-090-0

ISBN 978-1-47111-085-6

ISBN 978-1-47111-088-7

ISBN 978-1-47111-086-3

For more details please visit www.simonandschuster.co.uk